The fate of the African American community remains a central and hotly contested focus of our national dialogue. Although American race relations, and the structure of opportunities facing most African Americans, have improved dramatically in recent decades, daunting challenges and questions remain.

This book examines the vexing reality of racial conditions in America today: improved overall, but far more complicated than they used to seem, and in important respects continually depressing. Thirteen provocative and timely essays —by some of the most highly respected experts in the nation—present thoughtful, and often competing, assessments of African American progress and of the prospects for its further enhancement. The authors examine the educational achievement disparities and education policy choices confronting black America; the track record of faith-based organizations in improving poor inner-city communities; the continuing impediments to residential integration; and data-based arguments for continuing affirmative action programs.

The book concludes with a discussion of the feasibility of "reaching beyond race" to build stronger political coalitions for racially progressive policies.

the African American American Predicament

the African American Predicament

Christopher H. Foreman Jr.
Editor

BROOKINGS INSTITUTION PRESS
Washington, D.C.

ABOUT BROOKINGS

The Brookings Institution is a private nonprofit organization devoted to research, education, and publication on important issues of domestic and foreign policy. Its principal purpose is to bring knowledge to bear on current and emerging policy problems. The Institution maintains a position of neutrality on issues of public policy. Interpretations or conclusions in publications of the Brookings Institution Press should be understood to be solely those of the authors.

Library of Congress Cataloging-in-Publication data
The African American predicament / Christopher H. Foreman Jr., editor.
p.   cm.
Includes bibliographical references and index.
ISBN 0-8157-2880-8 (cloth)
1. Afro-Americans—Civil rights. 2. Afro-Americans—Social conditions—1975—3. United States—Race relations. 4. United States—Race relations—Forecasting. I. Foreman, Christopher H. Jr.
E185.615 .A5925 1999   99-6675
305.896'073—dc21   CIP

9 8 7 6 5 4 3 2 1

The paper used in this publication meets minimum requirements of the American National Standard for Information Sciences—-Permanence of Paper for Printed Library Materials: ANSI Z39.48-1984.

Typeset in Sabon and Futura

Composition by Peter Lindeman
Arlington, Virginia

Printed by R. R. Donnelley and Sons
Harrisonburg, Virginia

In memory of

James Farmer

1920–99

Acknowledgments

Everything has antecedents. The present volume was inspired by the spring 1998 issue of the *Brookings Review*, which presented a highly regarded, nine-article symposium on "Black America: Progress and Prospects." I am grateful to Tom Mann, then director of the Governmental Studies program, for encouraging me to serve as guest editor for that issue. Brenda Szittya, editor of the *Brookings Review*, proved an enthusiastic and immensely creative collaborator, unshakably determined to make that issue something special. My thanks go to Tom, to Brenda, and to President Michael Armacost for realizing that, at long last, Brookings ought to raise its profile on the sensitive and confounding but enduringly important matter of race. Funds generously provided by the David Woods Kemper Foundation enabled the work to go forward.

Crafting a new finished product from an older one might appear easy. And I had, after all, the considerable advantage of a first-rate foundation on which to build. But deciding on and reliably implementing changes, both large and small, proved as demanding as it was stimulating. Once again I could call on Brenda for timely assistance. But most of the day-to-day burden fell onto the capable shoulders of Pat Fowlkes, who typed endless revisions while keeping track of the multiple versions of each essay that were necessarily generated by give-and-take between authors and editor.

I am also grateful to Janet Walker, managing editor of the Brookings Press, for her calm and professional oversight of the book's publication. Susan Woollen, intuitively grasping the kind of "face" the book needed to present, worked with Terry Patton Rhoads to achieve the desired effect. The final manuscript was edited by Diane Hammond. Sherry Smith provided the index, and Kevin Manzel proofed the pages.

Finally, I should observe that the views expressed here are solely those of the various authors and should not be ascribed to the persons or institutions whose assistance is acknowledged above or to the trustees, officers, or other staff members of the Brookings Institution.

C.H.F.

Contents

part one

The Predicament

one

The Rough Road to Racial Uplift

Christopher H. Foreman Jr.

From the beginning, *civil rights* was a misleading term, perhaps an outright misnomer. The moral, legal, and rhetorical pursuit of collective rights of access was but an essential strategy in a multifront war for a much larger prize: the uplift of a people that had endured slavery and, afterward, the trials of subordinate caste status. Civil rights never meant just individual rights, any more than the initials NAACP denoted a National Association for the Advancement of Coherent Principles. Indeed, civil rights leaders and organizations have always known that they must pursue the vast and varied interests of their stigmatized and marginalized constituents by any available avenue. Rights were more a means than an end. If progress appears to have stalled, it is largely because the successive strategies embraced by champions of racial uplift have all encountered important practical and political limits. For the most part, these strategies have not so much failed as fallen victim to inevitable exhaustion and diminishing returns.

Virtually everyone recognizes that the strategy emphasizing legal access, which was pursued during a heroic civil rights golden age, has long since run its course. As textbooks today routinely teach, that phase of the struggle, begun in the courts in the 1930s, shifted the trajectory toward Congress a generation later as favorable public opinion, nurtured by a disciplined plea for simple justice and bouts of seg-regationist violence, made such a turn politically viable. The basic access argument was simple and therefore potent. Individuals ought not to be proscribed, purely for reasons of color, from plainly quotidian activities available to other citizens: voting for mayor, viewing a movie from a seat of one's choosing, wolfing down a cheeseburger at a dimestore lunch counter. The great majority of white Americans had no particular affec-tion for blacks but had never felt the need for separate water fountains and segregated buses. Such relatively petty outrages proved hard to defend outside the Deep South. Thankfully it has now been a long while since even most white southerners would have insisted that, say, Har-vard's distinguished Afro-Americanist Henry Louis Gates Jr. ought not teach at a "white" university in the South.

The high moral perch afforded by the access agenda, however, had stringent limits, which became apparent early. The formal doors to advancement might have been unlocked, perhaps even might have stood wide open, but how many black Americans would or could walk through them? An energetic young "Skip" Gates might march off to Yale, but how many others would follow, especially if all the university did was mail out a brochure to Harlem with a road map to New Haven enclosed? Legally desegregated schools and workplaces could not, by themselves, yield diverse student bodies and workforces, much less ensure equal grad-uation and promotion rates.

Not surprisingly, as far back as the 1960s, the access agenda was giv-ing way to rather less lofty haggles over dollars and numbers—which are still ongoing. Congress could target funds on a wide array of prob-lems, creating new legal authorities when favorable combinations of sup-port and indifference prevailed. A less openly democratic approach to African American uplift lay in the dull machinery of administration, amid the arcana of government regulations and guidance memoranda and sub-ject to policing by the courts. Merely offering individualized redress to particular claimants according to each specific grievance appeared dread-fully inadequate to the scale of the social challenge—rather like restor-ing a beach by hauling in one grain of sand at a time. More institutionally aggressive efforts, formal and informal, seemed warranted. Thus were born goals and timetables, minority contracting set-asides, and the entire regime of both hard (formal, mandated, quantitatively monitored) and soft (informal, voluntary, improvisational, hortatory) affirmative action.

As long ago as the mid-1960s, advocates for black uplift heard a new and disturbing thunder in the distance. Lightning struck in the form of the now-legendary government report crafted by Assistant Secretary of Labor Daniel Patrick Moynihan.[1] The Moynihan Report, as it came to be called, suggested serious tears in the black community's social fabric, which might widen with time. Neither a leadership anchored in the safe harbor of its access and affirmative action agenda nor the increasingly strident blacks gathering under the "black power" rubric were in any mood to hear some Irishman's embarrassing prattle about "Negro family structure," however plainly sympathetic and data laden. Social policy thinkers and researchers have been making up for considerable lost time as a result.

This diverse volume reflects a vexing reality. On racial matters, the American condition is overall dramatically improved but is far more complicated than it used to seem and, in important respects, continually depressing. As Gates reminds us in his essay on the two nations of black America, a significant black middle class has emerged (and not solely through affirmative action). White racial attitudes are astonishingly transformed from where they stood during Franklin Roosevelt's presidency, when the lynching of blacks was still an informally listed entrée on the menu of Deep South civic entertainments.

Tenacious ills remain, for which neither the pure right of access nor affirmative action is satisfactory medicine. One such problem is educational: significantly lower cognitive skills and test scores among minority youngsters, a problem explored with unprecedented care in the remarkable volume from which the chapter by Christopher Jencks and Meredith Phillips is drawn.[2] Scholars disagree about the influence of systemic resource disparities in creating and sustaining the gap in skills and scores. While Jencks and Phillips acknowledge some role for funding and other resource inequities, they also contend that this omits too much of the causal story, including preschool and out-of-school experiences. Alternatively, Linda Darling-Hammond strongly emphasizes the structure of educational opportunities offered by school systems. Darling-Hammond, Jencks, and Phillips agree on the salience of at least one key resource disparity: on average, black students tend to be taught by less-qualified teachers than white students. How would affirmative action remedy this problem? Indeed, one can easily anticipate the argument that affirmative action helps to sustain it. Frustration on this front has led to calls for making schools compete for students, a development that Paul Peterson and Jay Greene view favorably.

Other long-term challenges include teenage pregnancies (although recent trends inspire cautious optimism)[3] and the vastly disproportionate involvement of black males in the criminal justice system. With a keen appreciation of how the values that underlie behavior are forged and sustained, John DiIulio pleads (with eloquence, passion, and considerable data) that we attack such problems via the kind of faith-based institutions that have historically anchored black civic life. Although DiIulio is optimistic about the present and potential capacity of such institutions to transform minority residents (and thus their communities), his unstated premise is that the fates of these residents will play out mostly *within* existing locales. Nathan Glazer's pessimistic report on the persistence of residential segregation describes a primary underlying constraint facing anyone aspiring to improve quality of life, and life chances, among African Americans.

Clearly, employment (or the lack of it) remains central to the disparity in life chances between poor African Americans and other citizens. As Abigail and Stephan Thernstrom point out, black employment prospects began looking up a long time ago, well before the affirmative action era. Among the worst-off blacks, those whom William Julius Wilson famously labeled "the truly disadvantaged," unemployment is still rampant and is often manifested in almost complete disengagement from the world of work.[4] Job training and job-readiness coaching are often promoted and widely attempted; but they work unevenly, and least reliably, among the low-income youths who should have the most to gain from them.[5] On the other hand, job training has the considerable political virtue of remaining popular among blacks and whites alike.[6]

The widely touted unpopularity of affirmative action notwithstanding, Orlando Patterson offers two novel data-based arguments in its behalf. One is that it helps compensate for deficiencies in the social networks vital to sustaining employment (and other social) opportunities.

The other is that affirmative action in practice actually proves to be more popular than in the abstract.

Even if affirmative action were noncontroversial, various disparities between the races (in accumulated wealth, for example) would endure for a long time to come. Whatever white racism lingers today does not cause most of these difficulties. Moreover, the view that "nothing has fundamentally changed" on America's racial landscape is insupportable. In their book *America in Black and White: One Nation, Indivisible,* the Thernstroms opine that such a flat-earth view of white attitudes "can only be held by those who believe that social science evidence is worthless."[7] Actually, as they know, that is too simple an explanation for the widespread reliance on the rhetorical hammer of the term *racism*.

For many African Americans, the term may be an intuitively appealing way to make sense of a complicated and disturbing social milieu. Resort to this term (manifested most starkly in popular belief that antiblack conspiracies abound) appears symptomatic of a frustrated groping for answers to questions triggered, ironically, by the vanquishing of the old racial order and by the failure of newly open doors to reveal reliable pathways to equality. The burial of Jim Crow accompanied the emergence of problems that scarcely existed earlier, and this may help persuade some African Americans that a malicious chicanery must be afoot. In the bad old days, after all, a man with no schooling beyond the primary grades could far more easily feed his family. No one's worst nightmare would have included crack cocaine or gun-wielding children.

For advocates and the intelligentsia, "racism" offers obvious political leverage, a way to seize the moral high ground and press hard for social change. Although racist attitudes have dramatically abated in recent decades, more than enough manifestations of racism remain to offer both a plausible explanation for the black masses and a convenient advocacy fulcrum for black leadership. (NAACP board chairman Julian Bond's insistence that his organization battles "white supremacy" is mere inches away rhetorically.)

In the volume's final section, Paul Sniderman and Edward Carmines urge a quite different strategy of "reaching beyond race" to defend public policies helpful to African Americans. Drawing on a series of intriguing experiments, Sniderman and Carmines suggest that opposition to race-specific policies (even among racially tolerant whites) is anchored not in racism but in genuine moral misgivings about purely racial justifications. They want to sustain racially progressive policies with a more durable political coalition, and they believe it can be done. Philip Klinkner and Rogers Smith offer a more pessimistic assessment, grounded in their reading of America's dense racial history. Black progress and regress, they argue, is historically patterned, with identifiable social and political conditions favoring one or the other. Unfortunately, they suggest, conditions favoring progress are diminished or absent, while those leading to regress appear to be on the rise. Jennifer Hochschild ponders looming volatility in interethnic politics, with its prospects for both coalition and competition. Will African Americans advance in concert with other groups? Or will nascent tensions between blacks and other minorities blossom, hindering mutually beneficial alliances?

We need hard and courageous thinking about the complex array of troubles that plague the black community and the nation, but we do not suffer for lack of chatter about race. A careful empirical study of the amount of attention accorded race in both the electronic and print media would surely find an impressive amount of race-related news as well as opinion from every conceivable viewpoint. We may not always be completely forthright with one another, but the subject is never very far off any sentient citizen's radar screen. As Donald Horowitz remarked not long ago, Americans today may be enduring a serious case of "race fatigue."

We *do* lack both crucial knowledge (about how to produce various positive policy effects) and the political consensus essential to making available dramatically increased resources for any number of policy initiatives. As Glenn Loury suggests, we may lack something more profound: the sheer capacity to think about the problems of the black poor with the combination of complexity and sympathy they deserve and require. For Loury, America's history, its very way of life, is deeply implicated in a malaise from which many would too easily distance themselves. Possibly the worst effect of all the furor over affirmative action (whose main beneficiaries are middle class) is to shift the spotlight away from the most disadvantaged African Americans, those whose fates merit the most attention and the hardest thinking of all.

Notes

1. The report, officially known as *The Negro Family: The Case for National Action,* is reprinted in Lee Rainwater and William L. Yancey, *The Moynihan Report and the Politics of Controversy* (MIT Press, 1967).

2. Christopher Jencks and Meredith Phillips, eds., *The Black-White Test Score Gap* (Brookings, 1998).

3. Stephanie J. Ventura, T. J. Mathews, and Sally C. Curtin, "Declines in Teenage Birth Rates, 1991–97: National and State Patterns," *National Vital Statistics Reports* (Rockville, Md.: National Center for Health Statistics, 1998).

4. William Julius Wilson, *When Work Disappears: The New World of the Urban Poor* (Knopf, 1996).

5. Howard S. Bloom and others, "The Benefits and Costs of JTPA Title II-A Programs: Key Findings from the National Job Training Partnership Act Study," *Journal of Human Resources* 32 (Summer 1997), pp. 549–76. See also W. Norton Grubb, *Learning to Work: The Case for Reintegrating Job Training and Education* (New York: Russell Sage Foundation, 1996); Robert I. Lerman, "Building Hope, Skills, and Careers: Creating a Youth Apprenticeship System," in *Social Policies for Children,* edited by Irwin Garfinkel, Jennifer L. Hochschild, and Sara S. McLanahan (Brookings, 1996), pp. 136–72.

6. A December 1997 *New York Times*/CBS News Poll asked respondents whether they favored "government financing for job training for minorities to help them get ahead in industries where they are underrepresented." Sixty-four percent of whites and 95 percent of blacks favored such financing. See Sam Howe Verhovek, "In Poll, Americans Reject Means But Not Ends of Racial Diversity," *New York Times,* December 14, 1997.

7. Stephan Thernstrom and Abigail Thernstrom, *America in Black and White: One Nation, Indivisible* (Simon and Schuster, 1997), p. 500.

two

**The Two Nations
of Black America**

Henry Louis Gates Jr.

Six black men, each intellectually gifted in his own way, graduated from Yale College in the class of 1966. Each had managed, through some luck and a lot of pluck, to penetrate the ironclad barriers that had kept blacks matriculating at Yale to a fixed number for several decades. When I entered Yale two years later, ninety-five black men and women entered with me.

We were, to a person, caught up in the magic of the moment. Our good fortune was to have been selected to be part of the first "large" group of blacks included in Yale's commitment to educate "1,000 male leaders" each year, but we wondered, What would becoming a true black leader entail—for ourselves and for our people outside those walls? What sort of sacrifices and obligations did this special ticket to success bring with it? We worried about this—out loud and often.

Mostly we did our worrying in our long languid dinners in the colleges or in bull sessions in our suites, but our ritualized worrying space was our weekly meetings of the Black Student Alliance at Yale, headed by our black and shining prince, Glenn de Chabert. Our first item of business was always recruitment: how to get more black students to join us at New Haven. "This place is lily white," de Chabert would complain. "We are flies in the buttermilk." Brimming to overflowing with maybe two hundred students, the year's first meeting of the

BSAY looked like Harlem to me! I basked in the comfort of the range of brown colors in that room, but I also shuddered (as unnoticeably as I could) as I contemplated the awesome burden of leadership that we were made to feel in fulfilling our obligations to "help the community." After all, "the revolution" was unfolding around the country, and we, along with students like us at Harvard, Columbia, Princeton, Amherst, and Wesleyan, were to be its vanguard. This burden was no mere abstraction. The trial of New Haven's Black Panthers and of one of their leaders, Bobby Seale, was under way just a block or two away at New Haven's federal courthouse.

It astonishes me today how sharp my black colleagues were, how thoughtful beyond their years, how mature. For some reason, I long assumed that most of these guys were up from the ghetto, first-generation college. After all, our uniforms of the day, dashikis and blue jeans, obliterated our social distinctions. Names like Baskerville and Irving, Reed and Robinson, Schmoke and de Chabert, Barrington Parker III meant nothing particular to me. Only later would I discover that my contemporaries were no strangers to the idea of college. Had it not been for affirmative action, we would have met at Howard or Morehouse. They were not a new black middle-class bourgeoisie recruited to scale the ladder of class but the scions of an old and colored middle class recruited to integrate a white male elite. We clung to a soft black nationalist politics to keep ourselves on the straight and narrow.

For me, one crucial moment on the path of a more or less nationalist politics came while I was watching a black program that had been produced by students at Howard. In the film, a student, happily dating a white co-ed, comes to see the error of his ways after a campus visit by Maulana Ron Karenga. What a figure Karenga was—brown bald head, African robes, dark sunglasses. This was one bad dude, bad enough to make this guy in the film turn his back on love and come on home! I am not sure it had ever occurred to me before this that there was a way to be black, that one had to be in the program or outside of it.

Of course I knew what an Uncle Tom was, but even Uncle Tom was still part of the extended family. No one ever talked about banishing him from the tribe—before this—but this was a new day. A new generation, a vanguard within the vanguard of civil rights leadership, was demanding black power, the right to take over, and declaring venerable elders like Martin Luther King Jr. too old, too tired, too Milquetoast to be effective keepers of black power's incandescent fire. Dr. King was especially symptomatic, moving away as he had from an exclusively race-based politics to a more broadly conceived analysis that would bring poor people together. Where did a movement based on poverty leave all of us who were discovering an Afro-coifed, dashiki-clad blackness? Even the Black Panthers, Marxists that they claimed to be, manipulated the trappings of nationalist garb and rhetoric to maximize their appeal in a program that would eventually lead out of the black community and straight into a coalition with the brown and red and white truly poor.

J. Edgar Hoover and his FBI apparently were not aware of, or especially concerned about, what Freud called "the narcissism of tiny differences" within the black movement. For Hoover, the Panthers were black, they were radical, they were communist inspired—and they could be dealt with.

Systematic repression has a curious way of hampering the evolution of a movement. Not only were the Black Panthers repressed, Dr. King was assassinated—in retrospect the most dramatic act of violent repression in the wing of the movement that was beginning to embrace a class-based organizing principle that sought to reorder American society. Dr. King was killed. People like Huey Newton were imprisoned. People as unlike as Elijah Mohammed and Vernon Jordan, Jesse Jackson, and my new compatriots at Yale were being invited to integrate a newly expanded American upper middle class. The vanguard of black cultural nationalist political consciousness, in other words, became the vanguard in the race's broad movement across the great divide that had for so long prevented genuine economic mobility up the great American ladder of class.

Somehow, in the late sixties, in the aftermath of the King assassination, what was held to be authentically black began to change. Ghetto culture was valorized; the bourgeois life-style that the old-guard leaders of the civil rights establishment embodied was held to be too great a price to pay for our freedom—or at least to admit to. We wanted to be real, to be down with the people—to be successful, yes, but to be black at the same time. To be black was to be committed to a revolution of values, of mores and manners, of economic relationships. We were a people. The best way to dramatize this kinship was to dress, walk, and talk like a brother.

Above all, being black meant that we were at one with the revolution, standing firm in defense of the people and of that revolutionary vanguard, the persecuted and harassed Black Panther Party for Self-Defense. We went on strike on April 15, 1970, two weeks before Nixon and Henry Kissinger invaded Cambodia. We struck because Bobby Seale, we felt deeply, was not being tried fairly just down the street, bound and gagged as he was, at the worst moment of the trial. The strike rally was glorious. It seemed as if 100,000 people crowded onto the New Haven Green on May Day of 1970. Kingman Brewster, Yale's dynamic president, offered them food and shelter in the residential colleges. Each stained-glass window of the sacred cathedral of learning that we called Sterling stood intact at week's end. De Chabert had never spoken more impressively, never been more daring or inspiring.

However, graduation inevitably came, calling us to the newly expanded opportunities in graduate and professional schools and then on to similarly expanded opportunities in the broader professional and academic world. I went off to Cambridge, England, and when I returned a few years later to teach at Yale, so very much had changed. Any pretense that black admissions would be anything but staunchly and firmly middle class had ended during my absence. The new black middle class was perpetuating itself. Affirmative action, under assault by the Supreme Court's 1978 Bakke decision and wounded, still was functioning to increase the size of the middle class exponentially by a factor of four. Meanwhile, the gradual disappearance of industrial jobs in the cities was crippling that upwardly mobile class escalator that so many in the middle class had been able to ride.

Henceforth, in one of the most curious social transformations in the class structure in recent American history, two tributaries began to flow, running steadily into two distinct rivers of aspiration and achievement. By 1990, the black middle class, imperiled though it might have felt itself to be, had never been larger, more prosperous, or more relatively secure. Simultaneously, the pathological behavior that results from extended impoverishment engulfed a large part of a black underclass that seemed unable to benefit from an opening up of American society that the civil rights movement had long envisioned and had finally made possible, if only for some. For the first time ever, that inability to benefit seemed permanent.

Gangsterism became the handmaiden of hopelessness. Even middle-class children, well educated, often, and well heeled, found value in publicly celebrating a "gangsta" life-style. Cultural forms such as rap and hip hop, "the CNN of the black community," valorized violence, homophobia, misogyny, anti-Semitism, and a curious form of masochistic self-destruction. Then life began to imitate art—the gangsterism of the art of hip hop liberalized itself in the reciprocal murders of Tupac and Biggie Smalls—and the bizarre nightmare inversion of popular black values manifested itself in a most public way.

Which brings us to the present—for the African American community, the best of times and the worst of times. We have the largest black middle class in our history and the largest black underclass. In 1990, 2,280,000 black men were in prison, or on probation, or on parole, while 23,000 earned a college degree. That's a ratio of 99 to 1, compared with a ratio of 6 to 1 for white men.

What do we do about this? What do we not do?

First of all, we have to stop feeling guilty about our success. Too many of us have what psychologists call the guilt of the survivor: deep anxieties about leaving the rest of our fellow blacks in the inner city of despair. We need to feel a commitment to service, not to guilt. Our community and our families prepared us to be successful. "Get all the education you can," they told us over and over—and we did.

Second, we do not have to fail in order to be black—as odd as this sounds. Far too many young black kids say that succeeding is "white." Had any of us said this sort of thing when we were growing up, our families and friends would have checked us into a mental institution. We need more success, individually and collectively.

Third, we do not have to pretend any longer that 35 million people can ever possibly be members of the same economic class. The entire population of Canada is 30 million. Canadians are not all members of one economic class. Nor do they speak with one voice, united behind one single leader. As each of us knows, we have never been members of one social or economic class and never will be. The best we can strive for is that the class differentials within the black community—the bell curve of class—cease their lopsided ratios because of the pernicious nature of racial inequality.

So how do we do this? How do we "fight the power" in a post–civil rights world in which Bull Connor and George Wallace are no longer the easy targets? A world in which the rhetoric of the civil rights era sounds hollow and empty? A world in which race differences and class differentials have been ground together in a crucible of misery and squalor in such a way that few of us can tell where one stops and the other begins? I certainly have no magic cures.

We do, however, know that the causes of poverty within the black community are both structural and behavioral. Scholars as diverse as philosopher Cornel West and sociologist William Julius Wilson have pointed this out, and we are foolish to deny it. A household composed of a sixteen-year-old mother, a thirty-two-year-old grandmother, and a forty-eight-year-old great grandmother cannot possibly be a site for hope and optimism. Our task, it seems to me, is to lobby for those social programs that have been demonstrated to make a difference for those motivated to seize these expanded opportunities.

More important, we have to demand a structural change in this country, the equivalent of a Marshall Plan for the cities. We have to take people off welfare, train them for occupations relevant to a twenty-first-century, high-tech economy, and put them to work. Joblessness, as Wilson maintains, is our biggest crisis.

Although I favor such incentives as tax breaks to generate new investment in inner cities, youth apprenticeships with corporations, expanded tax credits for earned income, and tenant ownership of inner-city property, we have to face the reality that most of our inner cities are simply not going to become overnight oases of prosperity. We should think about moving black inner-city workers to the jobs rather than holding our breath waiting for new factories to resettle in the inner city.

It is only by confronting the twin realities of white racism, on the one hand, and our failures to take the initiative and break the cycle of poverty, on the other, that we, the remnants of W. E. B. Du Bois's talented tenth, will be able to assume a renewed leadership role for, and with, the black community. To continue to repeat the same old stale formulas; to blame "the man" for oppressing us all, in exactly the same ways; to scapegoat Koreans, Jews, or even Haitians for the failure of black Americans to seize local entrepreneurial opportunities is to fail to accept our role as leaders of our own community. Not to demand that each member of the black community accept individual responsibility for her or his behavior—whether that behavior assumes the form of black-on-black homicide, gang members violating the sanctity of the church, unprotected sexual activity, gangster rap lyrics, whatever—is for us to function merely as ethnic cheerleaders selling woof tickets from campus or suburbs, rather than saying the difficult things that may be unpopular with our fellows. Being a leader does not necessarily mean being loved; loving one's community means daring to risk estrangement and alienation from it in the short run in order to break the cycle of poverty and despair over the long run. What is at stake is nothing less than the survival of our country and of the African American people themselves.

Those of us on campus can also reach out to those of us left behind on the streets. The historically black colleges and universities and Afro-American studies departments in this country can institutionalize sophomore- and junior-year internships for community development through organizations such as the Children's Defense Fund. Together we can combat teenage pregnancies, black-on-black crime, the spread of AIDS from drug abuse and unprotected sexual relations, and counter the spread of despair and hopelessness in our communities. Dr. King did not die so that half of us would make it, half of us perish, forever tarnishing two centuries of agitation for our equal rights. We, the members of the talented tenth, must accept our historic responsibility and live Dr. King's credo that none of us is free until all of us are free; that all of us are brothers and sisters, as Dr. King said so long ago—white and black, Protestant and Catholic, Gentile and Jew and Muslim, rich and poor—even if we are not brothers-in-law.

three **The Legacy of Slavery**

Glenn C. Loury

The United States of America, "a new nation, conceived in liberty and dedicated to the proposition that all men are created equal," began as a slave society. What can rightly be called the original sin, slavery has left an indelible imprint on our nation's soul. A terrible price had to be paid, in a tragic, calamitous civil war, before this new democracy could be rid of that most undemocratic institution. For black Americans the end of slavery was just the beginning of our quest for democratic equality; another century would pass before the nation came fully to embrace that goal. Even now millions of Americans recognizably of African descent languish in societal backwaters. What does this say about our civic culture as we enter a new century?

The eminent Negro man of letters W. E. B. Du Bois predicted in 1903 that the issue of the twentieth century would be "the problem of the color line."[1] He has been proven right. At midcentury the astute Swedish observer of American affairs, Gunnar Myrdal, reiterated the point, declaring the race problem to be our great national dilemma and fretting about the threat it posed to the success of our democratic experiment.[2] Du Bois must have relished the irony of having a statue named Liberty oversee the arrival in New York's harbor of millions of foreigners, "tempest-tost" and "yearning to breathe free," even as black southern peasants—not alien, just profoundly alienated—were kept unfree at the social margins. Myrdal observed a racist ideology that openly questioned the Negro's human worth survive our defeat of the Nazis and abate only when the cold war rivalry made it intolerable that the "leader of the free world" should be seen to preside over a regime of racial subordination.

This sharp contrast between America's lofty ideals, on the one hand, and the seemingly permanent second-class status of the Negroes, on the other, put the onus on the nation's political elite to choose the nobility of their civic creed over the comfort of long-standing social arrangements. Ultimately they did so. Viewed in historic and cross-national perspective, the legal and political transformation of American race relations since World War II represents a remarkable achievement, powerfully confirming the virtue of our political institutions. Official segregation, which some southerners as late as 1960 were saying would live forever, is dead. The caste system of social domination enforced with open violence has been eradicated. Whereas two generations ago most Americans were indifferent or hostile to blacks' demands for equal citizenship rights, now the ideal of equal opportunity is upheld by our laws and universally embraced in our politics. A large and stable black middle class has emerged, and black participation in the economic, political, and cultural life of this country, at every level and in every venue, has expanded impressively. This is good news. In the final years of this traumatic, exhilarating century, it deserves to be celebrated.

Today's Race Problem

Nevertheless, as anyone even vaguely aware of the social conditions in contemporary America knows, we still face a "problem of the color line." The dream that race might some day become an insignificant category in our civic life now seems naively utopian. In cities across the country, and in rural areas of the Old South, the situation of the black underclass and, increasingly, of the black lower working classes is bad and getting worse. No well-informed person denies this, though there is debate over what can and should be done about it. Nor do serious people deny that the crime, drug addiction, family breakdown, unemployment, poor school performance, welfare dependency, and general decay in these communities constitute a blight on our society virtually unrivaled in scale and severity by anything to be found elsewhere in the industrial West.

What is sometimes denied, but what must be recognized, is that this is, indeed, a race problem. The plight of the underclass is not rightly seen as another (albeit severe) instance of economic inequality, American-style. These black ghetto dwellers are a people apart, susceptible to stereotyping, stigmatized for their cultural styles, isolated socially, experiencing an internalized sense of helplessness and despair, with limited access to communal networks of mutual assistance. Their purported criminality, sexual profligacy, and intellectual inadequacy are the frequent objects of public derision. In a word, they suffer a pariah status. It should not require enormous powers of perception to see how this degradation relates to the shameful history of black-white race relations in this country.

Moreover, there is a widening rift between blacks and whites who are not poor—a conflict of visions about the continuing importance of race in American life. Most blacks see race as still of fundamental importance; most whites (and also many Asians and Hispanics) think blacks are obsessed with race. This rift impedes the attainment of commonly shared, enthusiastically expressed civic ideals that might unite us across racial lines in efforts to grapple with our problems. The notion of the "beloved community," where blacks and whites transcend their differences and cooperate in universal brotherhood to foster racial integration, has never achieved broad appeal. As the sociologist William Julius Wilson stressed in 1978 in his misunderstood classic, *The Declining Significance of Race,* the locus of racial conflict in our society has moved from the economic to the social and political spheres.[3]

Indeed, one can almost see Du Bois's problem of the color line shifting before one's eyes, as a historic transformation on race-related issues in the United States is taking place. Arguments about black progress are but one part of the broader endeavor to recast our national understanding of racial matters—an undertaking of enormous importance. It has been a very long time since the civil rights movement constituted a force able to mold the nation's moral sensibilities. A struggle that succeeded brilliantly to win legal equality for blacks after a century of second-class citizenship has for the most part failed to win a national commitment toward eradicating the effects of this historical inheritance. The civil rights approach—petitioning the courts and the federal government for relief against the discriminatory treatment of private or state actors—reached its limit more than a decade ago. Deep improvement in the status of many blacks has taken place, even as the underclass has grown, and there seems to be no politically effective way of mobilizing a national assault on the remaining problems.

What is more, there has been profound demographic change in American society since the 1960s. During this period, nearly 20 million immigrants have arrived on our shores, mostly from non-European points of origin. Hispanics will soon be the nation's largest ethnic minority group. Asian American college students and urban entrepreneurs are more numerous and more important in the country's economic and political life than ever before. This development is making obsolete the old black-white framework, though blacks must occupy a unique position in any discussion of the nation's ethnic history. Nowadays, as a political matter, to focus solely on the old tension between blacks and whites is to miss something of basic importance.

It is against this backdrop that statistical analyses of the status of African Americans are being conducted. Assessing how much or how little progress has taken place for blacks, and why, is one of the most fiercely contested empirical issues in the social sciences. For years, liberal advocates of blacks' interests tried to deny that meaningful change was occurring. That assessment has always had problems, in my view. In any event, it is no longer tenable. Now the dominant voices on this subject come from right of center. They seem decidedly unfriendly to black aspirations. With great fanfare, these conservatives declare the historic battle against racial caste to have been won. They go on to say that, but for the behavioral dysfunction of the black poor and the misguided demands for affirmative action from a race-obsessed black middle class, our problem of the color line could be put behind us. Stephan and Abigail Thernstrom, in their book, *America in Black and White: One Nation, Indivisible,* offer a prime example of this mode of assessment.[4] This line of argument should not be permitted to shape our national understanding of these matters.

Rooted in History

A social scientist of any sophistication recognizes that societies are not amalgams of unrelated individuals creating themselves anew—out of whole cloth, as it were—in each generation. A complex web of social connections and a long train of historic influences interact to form the opportunities and shape the outlooks of individuals. Of course, individual effort is important, as is native talent and sheer luck, for determining how well or poorly a person does in life. Social background, cultural affinities, and communal influence are also of great significance. This is the grain of truth in the conservatives' insistence that cultural differences lie at the root of racial inequality in America. The deeper truth is that, for some three centuries now, the communal experience of the slaves and their descendants has been shaped by political, social, and economic institutions that, by any measure, must be seen as oppressive. When we look at underclass culture in the American cities of today we are seeing a product of that oppressive history. It is morally obtuse and scientifically naive to say, in the face of the despair, violence, and self-destructive folly of these people, that "if they would get their act together, like the poor Asian immigrants, then we would not have such a horrific problem in our cities."

The only decent response in the face of the "pathological" behavior of American history's losers is to conclude that, while we cannot change our ignoble past, we must not be indifferent to the contemporary suffering that is linked to that past. The self-limiting patterns of behavior among poor blacks, "which some commentators are so quick to trot out," are products not of some alien cultural imposition upon a pristine Euro-American canvas but, rather, of social, economic, and political practices deeply rooted in American history.[5] We should not ignore the behavioral problems of the underclass, but we should discuss and react to them as if we were talking about our own children, neighbors, and friends. This is an American tragedy, to which we should respond as we might to an epidemic of teen suicide, adolescent drunken driving, or HIV infection among homosexual males—that is, by embracing, not demonizing, the victims.

The problem with talk about black culture, black crime, and black illegitimacy as explanatory categories in the hands of the morally obtuse is that it becomes an exculpatory device, a way of avoiding a discussion of mutual obligation. It is a distressing fact about contemporary American politics that simply to make this point is to risk being dismissed as an apologist for the inexcusable behavior of the poor. The deeper moral failing lies with those who, declaring "we have done all we can," would wash their hands of the poor.

It is morally and intellectually superficial in the extreme to begin and end one's argument with the observation that the problems of the underclass are due to their high rates of criminal behavior and out-of-wedlock births and not to white racism. This is what political discourse assessing the status of blacks has come to. The highly ideological character of racial debate in America makes nuance and complexity almost impossible to sustain. While it may be true that the most debilitating impediments to advancement among the underclass derive from patterns of behavior that are self-limiting, it is also true that our history has dealt poor blacks a very bad hand. Yes, there must be change in these behaviors if progress is to be made. A commitment of support will also be required from the broader society to help these folks help themselves.

The conservatives deny this. They rationalize the nasty, brutish, and short lives of a sizable minority of the black population as reflecting blacks' deficiencies rather than revealing any flaw in our way of life. Nowhere is the ideological character of this stance more clearly revealed than in the conservatives' celebration of immigrant success, over and against native black failure. That nonwhite immigrants succeed is taken as a vindication of the system; that blacks fail is said to be due entirely to their own inadequacies. This is obscenely ahistorical. Frankly, I remain optimistic about the prospect that black teenagers, given greater opportunity, might respond with better behavior. What makes me pessimistic about our future is the spectacle of politically influential American intellectuals grasping at these cultural arguments as reason to abandon or ignore their moral responsibilities to those who are least fortunate in our society.

Color Is Not Irrelevant

The debate over affirmative action has also become quite ideological in tone. I have been a critic of affirmative action policies for more than fifteen years. I was among the first to stress how the use of racial preferences sheltered blacks from the challenge of competing on the merits in our society. I argued strenuously against the inclination of blacks to see affirmative action as a totem—a policy assumed to lie beyond the bounds of legitimate criticism, symbolizing the nation's commitment to "do the right thing" for black people. However, in the wake of a successful ballot initiative banning affirmative action in California, I now find it necessary to reiterate the old, and in my view still valid, arguments on behalf of explicit public efforts to reduce racial inequality.

The current campaign against preferences goes too far by turning what before Proposition 209 had been a reform movement into an abolitionists' crusade. In my view, race-based allocations of public contracts, explicit double standards in the workplace, and large disparities in the test scores of blacks and whites admitted to elite universities are unwise practices, deservedly under attack. The U.S. Army's programs to commission more black officers, the public funding of efforts to bring blacks into science and engineering, and the goal of public universities to retain some racial diversity in their student bodies are all defensible practices that should be retained. The mere fact that these efforts take race into account should be not disqualifying.

Affirmative action, however prudently employed, can never be anything more than a marginal instrument for addressing the nation's unfinished racial business. The proponents of colorblind policy who bill their crusade against preferences as the Second Coming of the civil rights movement display a ludicrous sense of priorities. They make a totem of ignoring race, even as the social isolation of the urban black poor reveals how important color continues to be in American society. Argument about the legality of the government's use of race only scratches the surface, because it fails to deal with the manifest significance of race in the private lives of Americans, black and white.

In the brave new dispensation, color is supposed to be irrelevant, yet everywhere we look in America, people are attending assiduously to race. The U.S. Census revealed that, among married people twenty-five to thirty-four years old in 1990, 70 percent of Asian women and 39 percent of Hispanic women, but only 2 percent of black women, had white husbands. Racially mixed church congregations are so rare that they make front-page news. So culturally isolated are black ghetto teens that linguists find their speech patterns to be converging across geographic distances, even as this emergent dialect grows increasingly dissimilar from the speech of poor whites living but a few miles away. Childless white couples travel to China in search of infants to adopt, while ghetto-born orphans go parentless. This is not to say that American society is irredeemably racist but merely to illustrate how deeply imbedded in the social consciousness of our nation is the racial otherness of blacks. No accounts of contemporary race relations should minimize this fact. Yet that is precisely what the colorblind crusaders do.

Consider the commonsense observation that, in this country, an army in which blacks are one-third of the enlisted personnel but only 3 percent of the officer corps is likely to function poorly. The U.S. Army cares about the number of black captains because it needs to sustain effective cooperation among its personnel across racial lines. That the racial identities of captains and corporals sometimes matter to the smooth functioning of a military institution is a deep fact about our society that cannot be wished away.

Monitoring the number of blacks promoted to the rank of captain and formulating policies to increase that number are activities that inherently involve taking account of some individuals' race, so radical critics of affirmative action must oppose this. Yet depending on how such activities are undertaken, they need not entail the promulgation of racial double standards, nor need they seem to declare, as a matter of official policy, that racial identity is a determinant of an individual's moral worth. As the military sociologist Charles Moskos is fond of pointing out, the army is the only place in American society where large numbers of whites routinely take orders from blacks.[6] So the irony is that the moral irrelevance of race, which the colorblind absolutists take as their highest principle, may be more evident in the U.S. Army than elsewhere in our society precisely because the government has been allowed to use race in the conduct of its military personnel policies.

Notes

1. W. E. B. Du Bois, *The Souls of Black Folk* (Fawcett, 1903), p. 23.

2. Gunnar Myrdal, *An American Dilemma: The Negro Problem and American Democracy* (Harper and Row, 1962).

3. William Julius Wilson, *The Declining Significance of Race* (University of Chicago Press, 1978).

4. Stephan Thernstrom and Abigail Thernstrom, *America in Black and White: One Nation, Indivisible* (Simon and Schuster, 1997).

5. Dinesh D'Souza, *The End of Racism* (Free Press, 1995).

6. Charles C. Moskos and John Sibley Butler, *All That We Can Be* (HarperCollins, 1996).

part two

Affirmative Action

four   **Black Progress**

Abigail Thernstrom
Stephan Thernstrom

First, let us contrast a few numbers:

—In 1940, 60 percent of employed black women worked as domestic servants; in 1999 that number was 2.2 percent (60 percent held white-collar jobs).

—In 1958, 44 percent of whites said they would move if a black family became their next door neighbor; today, the figure is 1 percent.

—In 1964, the year the great Civil Rights Act was passed, only 18 percent of whites claimed to have a friend who was black; today, 86 percent say they do, while 87 percent of blacks assert they have white friends.[1]

Startling facts? Not really—but mostly unknown. As *Washington Post* columnist William Raspberry noted on August 7, 1998, "virtually the entire civil rights leadership has been hell-bent on proving that both the passing of the era of oppression and the dawning of a new era are myths. . . . It has become a virtual heresy in black America to acknowledge progress."

What a remarkable state of affairs: civil rights representatives determined to deny the racial progress for which they and their predecessors worked so long, so hard, and so successfully. To admit dramatic change, they seem to believe, is to invite white indifference, as if everything blacks now have is the consequence of white effort built on the fragile foundation of shame.[2]

Their resolve to conceal the obvious has had its intended effect. Allegedly dangerous optimism has been kept at bay. Although (as the Raspberry column suggests) the once solidly pessimistic front now contains cracks, gloom still characterizes the black voices most often heard in the media. Thus in July 1998 Bill Cosby's wife, Camille, writing on the murder of their son, described racism as "ominipresent and eternalized in America's institutions, media, and myriad entities."[3] A month earlier John Hope Franklin, head of President Clinton's national advisory board on race, described the brutal murder of a black man in Jasper, Texas, as "not all that much of an aberration." He went on: "We have at least several incidents like that every year."[4] The previous fall he had described a nation in which "every time people take a breath, it's in terms of color." Race consciousness—if not outright racism—is as American as apple pie.[5]

Undoubtedly traumatized by the horrors of the past, Franklin cannot see the world in which he lives today. Although race is still the American dilemma, and true racial equality remains an unfulfilled dream, America has changed. In Jasper itself and across the nation, whites and blacks alike were appalled by the news of the Texas murder; only the lunatic fringe now condones racially motivated violence. "Everywhere we look, we see clear racial fault lines that divide America now as much as in the past," Julian Bond said at a January 18, 1999, service commemorating the birthday of Martin Luther King Jr., even though Bond's rapt, standing-room-only audience was largely white.[6] None of these facts should come as a surprise. By 1997, a Gallup poll found, 83 percent of whites aged eighteen to thirty-four approved of interracial marriage. (The figure for blacks in the same age bracket was 86 percent.) Only 12 percent of whites objected to sending their children to a school in which more than half the students were black.[7] As the data suggest, only a small minority of whites have no black friends, and one has to look hard to find a white who objects to a black family living next door.

Both the racial climate and the status of blacks has changed. More than 40 percent of African Americans now consider themselves members of the middle class. Forty-two percent own their own homes, a figure that rises to 75 percent if we look just at black married couples. Black two-parent families earn only 13 percent less than those who are white. Almost a third of the black population lives in suburbia. Because these are facts the media seldom report, the black underclass too often defines black America—especially, it seems, to African Americans themselves. In a 1991 Gallup poll, about one-fifth of all whites, but almost half of black respondents, said that at least three of four African Americans were impoverished urban residents, by implication living in ghettos, in high-rise public housing projects, with crime and the welfare check as their main source of income. Yet in fact blacks who consider themselves to be middle class outnumber by a wide margin those with incomes below the poverty line.[8]

Fifty years ago most blacks were indeed trapped in poverty, although they did not mainly reside in inner cities. When Gunnar Myrdal published *An American Dilemma* in 1944, most blacks lived in the South and on the land, as laborers and sharecroppers. (Only one in eight owned the land on which he worked.) A trivial 5 percent of black men nationally were engaged in nonmanual, white-collar work of any kind; the vast majority held ill-paid, insecure, manual jobs—jobs that few whites would take. As noted, six of ten African American women were household servants who, driven by economic desperation, often worked twelve-hour days for pathetically low wages. Segregation in the South and discrimination in the North did create a sheltered market for some black businesses (funeral homes, beauty parlors, and the like) that served a black community barred from patronizing "white" establishments, but the number was minuscule.[9]

Beginning in the 1940s, however, deep demographic and economic change, accompanied by a marked shift in white racial attitudes, started blacks down the road to much greater equality. New Deal legislation that set minimum wages and hours and eliminated the incentive of southern employers to hire low-wage black workers put a damper on further industrial development in the region. In addition, the trend toward mechanized agriculture and a diminished demand for American cotton in the face of international competition combined to displace blacks from land. As a consequence, with the shortage of workers in northern manufacturing plants following the outbreak of World War II, south-

ern blacks in search of jobs boarded trains and buses in a great migration that lasted through the mid-1960s. They found what they were
looking for: wages so strikingly high in the North that in 1953 the average income for a black family was almost twice that of those who
remained in the South. Through much of the 1950s wages rose steadily
and unemployment was low.

By 1960 only one of seven black men still labored on the land; almost
a quarter were in white-collar or skilled manual occupations, and another
24 percent had semiskilled factory jobs, which meant membership in the
stable working class. The proportion of black women working as servants had been cut in half. Even those who did not move up into higher-
ranking jobs were doing much better.[10]

A decade later the gains were even more striking. Between 1940 and
1970, black men cut the income gap by about a third, and by 1970 they
were earning (on average) roughly 60 percent of what white men took
in. The advancement of black women was even more impressive. Black
life expectancy went up dramatically, as did black homeownership rates.
Black college enrollment also rose; by 1970 it was about 10 percent of
the total, three times the prewar figure. In subsequent years these trends
continued, although at a more leisurely pace. For instance, today more
than 30 percent of black men and nearly 60 percent of black women
hold white-collar jobs. Whereas in 1970 only 2.2 percent of American
physicians were black, the figure is now 4.5 percent. While the fraction
of black families with middle-class incomes rose almost forty points
between 1940 and 1970, it has inched up only another ten points since
then.[11]

The rapid change in the status of blacks for several decades followed
by a slowdown beginning just when racial preferences got their start
suggests that race-conscious strategies enjoy an inflated reputation. Yet
the assumption that racial preferences have been not only morally justified but effective—indeed, essential to black progress—has become the
conventional wisdom among the chattering classes. "Race-sensitive"
admissions in the nation's elite colleges and universities have created "the
backbone of the emergent black middle class," William G. Bowen and
Derek Bok argue in their much-celebrated book, The Shape of the River.[12]
It is a remarkably ahistorical claim; the black middle class was emerg-

ing rapidly in the era before affirmative action; black economic progress, as noted, began in the 1940s.

Black economic progress is a train that left the station more than fifty years ago, and it has been chugging along ever since. The elite colleges have played only a limited role in that progress. Look at lists of black professors, military officers, the chief executive officers of leading businesses, federal officials, and MacArthur Foundation "genius" award recipients: relatively few went to schools such as Yale and Duke and Haverford. We know, for instance, that the historically black colleges— not the elite schools that Bowen and Bok studied—have been most successful in turning out students who go on to get Ph.Ds.[13]

In general, the benefits of race-conscious policies appear much more limited than their advocates suggest. The greatest economic gains for African Americans since the early 1960s were in the years 1965 to 1975 and occurred mainly in the South. The economists John J. Donahue III and James Heckman discovered "virtually no improvement" in the wages of black men relative to those of white men outside the South over the entire period from 1963 to 1987 and attribute most southern gains to the powerful antidiscrimination provisions of the 1964 Civil Rights Act.[14]

Federal, state, and municipal set-asides are designed to promote black entrepreneurship, but their benefits appear to have been oversold. In 1994, the state of Maryland decided that at least 10 percent of the contracts it awarded would go to minority- and female-owned firms. The program "worked" if the goal was merely the narrow one of dispensing cash to designated groups. The questions, however, are whether government-sheltered businesses survive over the long term without extraordinary protection from free-market competition and whether they have any impact on the level of black poverty. On neither score is the picture reassuring. Programs are often fraudulent, with white contractors offering minority firms 15 percent of the profit with no obligation to do any of the work. Or the programs enrich those with the right connections who are already in a position to obtain government business. In Richmond, Virginia, for instance, the main effect of the ordinance was a working alliance between the economically privileged of both races. The white business elite signed on to a piece of the pie for blacks in order to polish its image as socially conscious and to secure support for the downtown revitalization it wanted. Black politicians used the bargain to suggest their own importance to low-income constituents, for whom the set-asides actually did little. Neither the white business elite nor the black politicians cared whether the policy in fact provided real economic benefits for ordinary working people—and it did not.[15]

Bowen and Bok focused exclusively on the creation of the black middle class through the mechanism of preferences in the nation's elite colleges. Their book "provides striking confirmation of the success of affirmative action in opening opportunities and creating a whole generation of black professionals," the *New York Times* announced in an editorial endorsing the book's conclusions.[16] Preferential admissions at highly selective colleges like Stanford, Emory, and Oberlin, the argument runs, create a pool of black graduates who then become the lawyers and doctors who form the "backbone" of the black middle class.

This is much too large a claim. The number of black college and university professors more than doubled between 1970 and 1990, the number of physicians tripled, the number of engineers almost quadrupled, and the number of attorneys increased more than sixfold. Although preferences (racial double standards for admission to institutions of higher education) may have played some role, the black professional class had been growing steadily in the prepreference decades of the 1940s through the 1960s. How can we be sure that the trends of those years would not have continued without preferences? Preferences at elite schools are not creating a new black middle class. In fact, black students at such schools generally come from families who already are middle class. Sixty-four percent of those in the Bowen and Bok study had at least one parent who graduated from college (among all black youths of college age, the comparable figure is 11 percent), and only 20 percent came from families with incomes of less than $22,000 (although nationally, half of all college-age African Americans fall into that category).[17] In any case, preferences in elite colleges (which affect only a relatively small number of black students) cannot possibly account for the strength of a middle class that is 44 percent of the nation's black population. The numbers simply do not add up.

For these and other reasons, Bowen and Bok's assertion that racial preferences at highly selective colleges and universities are rich in benefits and cost free does not withstand close scrutiny. The authors studied twenty-eight elite schools, looking at five particularly closely. On average, black students did relatively poorly in the classroom; their cumulative grade point average put them at the twenty-third percentile in their class—and even that figure is deceptively rosy.[18] If Bowen and Bok had differentiated between black students admitted regularly (about half of the total) and those admitted preferentially, they would likely have found the beneficiaries of preferences doing even worse.

Relatively poor academic performance was inevitable, given the decidedly weaker credentials that black students brought to the classroom. Among the 1989 admittees to the five colleges for which Bowen and Bok had the most extensive data, 19 percent of whites and 60 percent of blacks of applicants with combined SAT scores of 1,200 to 1,249 were accepted. In the next bracket up (1,250–99), 24 percent of whites but 75 percent of blacks were accepted; in the 1,500-or-better category, more than a third of whites were turned down, while every single black applicant got in. Schools at which the average white or Asian student has SAT scores in the top 3 to 4 percent of all test takers in the nation have been accepting black students with average scores at the seventy-fifth percentile, as well as lower high school grade point averages.[19]

Lower grades (on average) are not the only cost; black students do not graduate at the same rate as whites and Asians. Bowen and Bok stress the fact that almost eight of ten black students at the twenty-eight highly selective schools they studied did finish (double the national average for blacks). Flip the coin and look at the dropout rates, which they ignore. Only 6.3 percent of the whites in their 1989 sample failed to get a bachelors' degree (from any school), as compared with 20.8 percent of the African Americans. Hence the black dropout rate was 3.3 times the white rate, a much larger differential than the overall national gap. Furthermore, the racial difference widened as the selectivity of the school increased. The ratio of black to white dropout rates was 2.8 at the least selective of the twenty-eight colleges, 3.6 at those ranked in a middle group, and 4.2 at the very top.[20]

When black students (on average) do not do well academically, it creates or reinforces negative stereotypes about their intellectual capacity. Bowen and Bok claim to have found no evidence of the sort of white skepticism and black insecurity that has the potential to poison race relations and cripple talented African American students. Their surveys, however, barely scratch the surface of the problem. Although the authors make much of interracial friendships on campus, they never compare their findings to data that show that such friendships have become common in American society as a whole. The black graduates of the elite colleges they studied did have the confidence to move on to professional schools and prestigious occupations, but again, the authors fail to tell the whole story. Professional schools also admit students by glaring racial double standards. The preferentially admitted students at Northwestern or Williams do not catch up with their academically better prepared peers, and thus college preferences become preferences in graduate and professional schools as well.

The story of racial preferences in law school admissions is particularly well documented; we know for instance that 80 percent of black students accepted for the fall 1991 class had grades and test scores that, if they had been white, would have led to their being rejected by the school that admitted them.[21] At the most selective and prestigious schools, 17.5 times as many black students were admitted as would have been the case if academic qualifications alone had been taken into account. We also know that 43 percent of the preferentially admitted black law students either did not graduate or failed the bar exam after as many as six tries over three years. Further, it is far from clear that most of the 57 percent who did become lawyers are newcomers to the black middle class. Bowen and Bok argue that attendance at a highly selective college is the make-or-break ticket that gets black students into a good law school or other professional school and thus into the middle class. However, most of the African American students at their elite schools came from relatively well-off families. Their brand-name educations may give them an added advantage in entering the labor market or applying to professional schools, but they are unlikely candidates anyway for working-class status.

Racial preferences have not created the backbone of the black middle class nor have they done anything to attack black poverty. Preferential policies took shape in the late 1960s and early 1970s, when 30 percent of black families lived below the poverty line; in the three decades since, that figure has dropped only a few percentage points. "There are those who say, my fellow Americans, that even good affirmative action programs are no longer needed," President Clinton said in July 1995. "Let us consider" that "the unemployment rate for African Americans remains about twice that of whites."[22] Racial preferences were the president's answer to persistent inequality, although a quarter century of affirmative action had done nothing whatever to close the unemployment gap.

Persistent inequality is obviously serious, and if discrimination were the primary problem, then race-conscious remedies might be appropriate. In 1964 white racism was central to the story, but the picture is much more complicated now. Today blacks and whites graduate at the same rate from high school and are almost equally likely to attend college, yet on average they are not equally educated. Looking at years of schooling in assessing the racial gap in family income tells us little about the cognitive skills that whites and blacks bring to the job market; and cognitive skills affect earnings.

The National Assessment of Educational Progress (NAEP) is the nation's report card on what American students attending elementary and secondary schools know. Those tests show that African American students, on average, are alarmingly far behind whites in math, science, reading, and writing. For instance, black students at the end of their high school career are roughly four years behind white students in reading; the gap is comparable in other subjects.[23] A study of men aged twenty-six to thirty-three years who held full-time jobs in 1991 found that when education was measured by years of school completed, blacks earned 19 percent less than comparably educated whites, but that when word knowledge, paragraph comprehension, arithmetical reasoning, and mathematical knowledge were used as the yardstick of educational attainment, the results were reversed. Black men earned 9 percent *more* than white men with the same performance on basic tests.[24]

Other research suggests much the same. For instance, the work of economists Richard J. Murnane and Frank Levy demonstrates the increasing importance of cognitive skills in our changing economy. Employers in firms like Honda now require employees to read and do math problems at the ninth-grade level, at a minimum; the 1992 NAEP math tests reveal that only 22 percent of African American high school seniors (but 58 percent of their white classmates) were numerate enough for such firms to consider hiring them. In reading, 47 percent of whites but only 18 percent of African Americans could handle the printed word well enough to be employable in a modern automobile plant. Murnane and Levy find a clear impact on income; not years spent in school but strong skills make for high long-term earnings.[25]

Why is there such a glaring racial gap in levels of educational attainment? It is not easy to say. The gap, in itself, is very bad news, but even more alarming is the fact that it has been widening in recent years. In 1971, the average African American seventeen-year-old could read no better than the typical white child of eleven. The racial gap in math in 1973 was 4.3 years; in science in 1970 it was 4.7 years. By the late 1980s, however, the picture was notably brighter. Black students in their final year of high school were only 2.5 years behind whites in both reading and math and 2.1 years behind on tests of writing skills.[26] Had the trends of those years continued, by today black pupils would be performing about as well as their white classmates. Instead, black progress came to a halt, and serious backsliding began. Between 1988 and 1994, the racial gap in reading grew from 2.5 to 3.9 years; between 1990 and 1994, the racial gap in math increased from 2.5 to 3.4 years. In both science and writing, the racial gap has widened by a full year.

There is no obvious explanation for this alarming turnaround. The early gains doubtless had much to do with the growth of the black middle class, but the black middle class did not suddenly begin to shrink in the late 1980s. The poverty rate was not dropping significantly when educational progress was occurring, nor was it on the increase when the racial gap began once again to widen. The huge rise in out-of-wedlock births and the steep and steady decline in the proportion of black children growing up with two parents do not explain the fluctuating educational performance of African American children. The disintegration of the black nuclear family—presciently noted by Daniel Patrick Moynihan as early as 1965—was occurring rapidly in the period in which black scores were rising. Thus it cannot be invoked as the main explanation as to why scores began to fall many years later.

Some argue that the initial educational gains were the result of increased racial integration and the growth of such federal programs as Head Start and Title I, even though neither desegregation nor compensatory education seem to have increased the cognitive skills of the black children exposed to them. In any case, the racial mix in the typical school has not changed in recent years, and the number of students in compensatory programs and the dollars spent on them has kept going up.

What about changes in the curriculum and patterns of course selection by students? The educational reform movement that began in the late 1970s did succeed in pushing students into a "new basics" core curriculum that includes more English, science, math, and social studies courses. There is good reason to believe that taking tougher courses contributed to the temporary rise in black test scores, but this explanation, too, nicely fits the facts for the period before the late 1980s but not the very different picture thereafter. The number of black students going through new basics courses did not decline after 1988, which might have lowered their NAEP scores.

We are left with three tentative suggestions. First, the increased violence and disorder of inner-city lives that came with the introduction of crack cocaine and the drug-related gang wars of the mid-1980s might have affected black educational progress. Chaos in the streets and the schools affects learning inside and outside the classroom. In addition, an educational culture that has increasingly turned teachers into guides who help children explore whatever interests them may have affected black academic performance. As the educational critic E. D. Hirsch Jr. points out, the "deep aversion to and contempt for factual knowledge that pervade the thinking of American educators" lead to students failing to build the "intellectual capital" that is the foundation of all further learning.[27] That is particularly true of students who come to school most academically disadvantaged—those whose homes are not, in effect, an additional school. The deficiencies of American education hit hardest those most in need of that education.

Yet in the name of racial sensitivity, advocates for minority students dismiss both common academic standards and standardized tests. Such advocates have plenty of company in high places. For instance, Christopher Edley Jr., a professor of law at Harvard, a member of the U.S. Commission on Civil Rights, and President Clinton's point man on affirmative action has allied himself with testing critics. "The challenge for higher education leaders," he has said, "is to understand that these simple grids and indices are a bad way to think about merit."[28] Likewise, in May 1999 the Office of Civil Rights (OCR) in the U.S. Department of Education issued guidelines warning of the potentially discriminatory impact of "high-stakes testing."[29] OCR can encourage the abolition of tests at every grade level (or the use of racial double standards in grading those assessments) and the disparity in basic skills will indeed become less evident. But that will only make the problem harder to correct.

Closing that skills gap is obviously the first task if black advancement is to continue at its once fast pace. On the map of racial progress, education is the name of almost every road. Raise the level of black educational performance, and the gap in college graduation rates, in attendance at selective professional schools, and in earnings is likely to close as well. Moreover, with racial parity in achievement levels at age seventeen, the deeply divisive issue of racial preferences in higher education simply disappears.

Black progress over the last half century has been impressive, conventional wisdom to the contrary notwithstanding, but the nation has many miles still to go on the road to true racial equality. "I wish I could say that racism and prejudice were only distant memories . . . but as I look around I see that even educated whites and African-Americans have . . . lost hope in equality," Thurgood Marshall said in 1992. In fact, all hope has not been "lost," but certainly in the 1960s the civil rights community failed to anticipate just how long and difficult the voyage would be. (Thurgood Marshall envisioned an end to all school segregation within five years of the Supreme Court's decision in *Brown* v. *Board of Education*.) Many, particularly blacks, are now discouraged. A 1997 Gallup poll found a sharp decline in optimism since 1980; only 33 percent of blacks (versus 58 percent of whites) thought both the quality of life for blacks and race relations had gotten better over the previous decade.[30]

Thus progress—by many measures seemingly so clear—is dismissed as illusory. The ahistorical sense of nothing gained is in itself bad news. Pessimism is a self-fulfilling prophecy. If all our efforts as a nation to resolve the "American dilemma" have been in vain—if we have been spinning our wheels in the rut of ubiquitous and permanent racism, as Derrick Bell, Andrew Hacker, and others argue—then racial equality is an unattainable ideal.[31] If blacks and whites understand and celebrate the gains of the past, however, we will move forward with the optimism, insight, and energy that further progress surely demands.

Notes

1. Data are from Stephan Thernstrom and Abigail Thernstrom, *America in Black and White: One Nation, Indivisible* (Simon and Schuster, 1997).

2. White shame and its connection to racial preferences and other race-based public policies is discussed perceptively by Shelby Steele, *A Dream Deferred: The Second Betrayal of Black Freedom in America* (HarperCollins, 1998).

3. Camille Cosby, "America Taught My Son's Killer to Hate African-Americans," *USA Today,* July 8, 1998, p. 15A.

4. Kathy Lewis, "Race Panel Chairman Calls Jasper Slaying 'Abhorrent,'" *Dallas Morning News,* June 19, 1998, p. 4A.

5. Susan Page, "Race Panel Head Sees Progress, Backsliding," *USA Today,* November 17, 1997, p. A8.

6. Patricia J. Mays, "King Remembered at Church Services," Associated Press Online, January 19, 1999.

7. *Black/White Relations in the United States: A Gallup Poll Social Audit* (June 1997), slide 16 on their web site posting.

8. See Thernstrom and Thernstrom, *America in Black and White,* pp. 184, 197, 199–200, 211. The April 23–25, 1991, *Newsweek* Poll, Gallup Organization World Headquarters, April 26, 1991. In 1991, only 56 percent of blacks lived in central cities; 35 percent of them—6,163,000 persons (or 20 percent of the total African American population)—had incomes below the poverty line. U.S. Bureau of the Census, *The Black Population in the United States: March 1992,* Current Population Report P-20-471 (Government Printing Office, 1993), table 15.

9. Gunnar Myrdal, *An American Dilemma: The Negro Problem and American Democracy* (Harper, 1944). For a picture of black life in 1940 see Thernstrom and Thernstrom, *America in Black and White*, chaps. 1 and 2.

10. Thernstrom and Thernstrom, *America in Black and White*, chap. 3.

11. Ibid., chap. 7. For the data on white-collar jobs, see table 1; for the data on black physicians, see table 2; for the data on middle-class income, see table 7.

12. William G. Bowen and Derek Bok, *The Shape of the River: Long-Term Consequences of Considering Race in College and University Admissions* (Princeton University Press, 1998), p. 116. For a thorough critical appraisal, see Stephan Thernstrom and Abigail Thernstrom, "Reflections on *The Shape of the River*," *UCLA Law Review* (June 1999).

13. On black military officers, see Michael T. Nettles, ed., *The Transition from School to College and School to Work* (Fairfax, Va.: Frederick D. Patterson Research Institute of the College Fund/UNCF, 1997), p. 193. The MacArthur recipients are listed in the *Journal of Blacks in Higher Education*, no. 20 (1998), p. 31. On black Ph.D.s see the 1996 National Research Council, *Summary Report, 1996: Doctorate Recipients from United States Universities* (Washington, D.C.: National Academy Press, 1998), p. 42. For more evidence on this issue, see Thernstrom and Thernstrom, "Reflections on *The Shape of the River*."

14. John J. Donahue III and James Heckman, "Continuous versus Episodic Change: The Impact of Civil Rights Policy on the Economic Status of Blacks," *Journal of Economic Literature* 29 (1991), pp. 1603–43.

15. On the efficacy of the Maryland program, see Thomas W. Waldron, "Glendenning Calls Maryland's Minority Business Set-Aside Program 'Sham,'" *Baltimore Sun*, August 18, 1994, p. 3B. See also Timothy Bates and Darrell Williams, "Preferential Procurement Programs and Minority-Owned Business," *Journal of Urban Affairs* 17 (1995), pp. 1–17; George LaNoue, "Social Science and Minority Set-Aside," *Public Interest* (Winter 1993). The Richmond story is told in W. Avon Drake and Robert D. Holsworth, *Affirmative Action and the Stalled Quest for Black Progress* (University of Illinois Press, 1996). Tamar Jacoby's *Someone Else's House: America's Unfinished Struggle for Integration* (Free Press, 1998), Part III, offers grounds for similar skepticism about the effects of such programs in Atlanta.

16. Editorial, "The Facts about Affirmative Action," *New York Times*, September 14, 1998, p. A32.

17. Bowen and Bok, *The Shape of the River*, pp. 49, 341.

18. Ibid., p. 72. The authors refer to this fact as "troubling" and devote sixteen pages to a discussion of what they term the underperformance of black students (pp. 72–88). Their treatment of this issue, though, is extremely bland and low-keyed, and they seem to forget about the matter altogether when they sum up the broad conclusions of their work. Thus their verdict in the penultimate chapter is that "the data assembled in this volume should dispel any impression that the abilities and

performance of the selective colleges and universities have been disappointing" (p. 56). Their evidence about the academic performance of preferentially admitted students is "troubling" but not "disappointing." It is instructive to compare their work on this point with a chapter written by William Bowen and a collaborator for another volume; see Frederick E. Vars and William G. Bowen, "Scholastic Aptitude Test Scores, Race, and Academic Performance in Selective Colleges and Universities," in *The Black-White Test Score Gap*, edited by Christopher Jencks and Meredith Phillips (Brookings, 1998), pp. 457–79. Vars and Bowen call black underperformance an issue that "is crucial to face," sounding a note of alarm notably missing from the complacent pages of *The Shape of the River*. Attempting to persuade a broad audience of the merits of preferential policies, Bowen and Bok put a much more benign spin on the same findings.

19. Bowen and Bok, *The Shape of the River*, figure 2.5.

20. Calculated from ibid., table D.3.1; data on bachelor's degree from ibid., figure 2.5; data on dropout rate from ibid., table D.3.2. Bowen and Bok calculate two graduation rates, a "first-school" rate for those who take a degree at the college they first enter and an overall rate, which includes those who drop out of their first school but who do graduate from some institution. Perhaps the best data on graduation rates broken down by race are from the National Collegiate Athletic Association (NCAA), which publishes an annual report on students attending one of the 308 Division I schools. One report indicates that 40 percent of the black freshmen who enrolled in an NCAA Division I school in 1991–92 earned a bachelor's degree by 1998. The figure for whites is 58 percent.

21. This discussion of the law school picture is taken from Stephan Thernstrom, "Diversity and Meritocracy in Legal Education: A Critical Evaluation of Linda F. Wightman's 'The Threat to Diversity in Legal Education,'" *Constitutional Commentary* 15 (1998), pp. 11–43.

22. Speech by President Clinton July 19, 1995, extended excerpts from which were reprinted in the *Washington Post*, July 20, 1995, p. A12.

23. The NAEP data for 1971–94 are summarized in Thernstrom and Thernstrom, *America in Black and White*, p. 355. For more recent data, see National Center for Education Statistics, *NAEP 1996 Trends in Academic Progress* (U.S. Department of Education, 1997). The racial gap documented in *America in Black and White* continued to widen between 1994 and 1996.

24. George Farkas and Keven Vicknair, "Appropriate Tests of Racial Wage Discrimination Require Controls for Cognitive Skills: Comment on Cancio, Evans, and Maume," *American Sociological Review* 61 (1996), pp. 557–60. This is a critique of A. Silvia Cancio, T. David Evans, and David J. Maume, "Reconsidering the Declining Significance of Race: Racial Differences in Early Career Wages," in the same issue of the *American Sociological Review*, pp. 541–56, which measures education crudely by levels of schooling completed. The authors' rejoinder to this cri-

tique in the same issue, pp. 561–64, argues that it is inappropriate to control for education by using tests of cognitive skills because they only test "exposure to the values and experiences of the White middle class" (p. 561).

25. Richard J. Murnane and Frank Levy, *Teaching the New Basic Skills: Principles for Educating Children to Thrive in a Changing Economy* (Free Press, 1996), pp. 32, 41–44. A more detailed technical version of the analysis is available in Richard Murnane, John Willett, and Frank Levy, "The Growing Importance of Cognitive Skills in Wage Determination," *Review of Economics and Statistics* 77 (1995), pp. 251–66.

26. The data on changes in the racial gap in academic performance can be found in Thernstrom and Thernstrom, *America in Black and White*, pp. 352–62.

27. E. D. Hirsch Jr., *The Schools We Need and Why We Don't Have Them* (Doubleday, 1996), pp. 43, 54.

28. Quoted in Ethan Bronner, "A Special Report: Colleges Look for Answers to Racial Gaps in Testing," *New York Times*, November 8, 1997, p. A1.

29. For a discussion of the OCR guidelines, see Abigail Thernstrom, "Testing, the Easy Target," op-ed, *New York Times*, June 10, 1999, p. A31.

30. *Black/White Relations in the United States: A Gallup Poll Social Audit* (June 1997). See also "Marshall Receives Award," *Houston Chronicle*, July 5, 1993, p. 10; "NAACP Sets Advanced Goals," *New York Times*, May 18, 1954, p. 16, as quoted in Gerald N. Rosenberg, *The Hollow Hope: Can Courts Bring about Social Change?* (University of Chicago Press, 1991), p. 43.

31. Derek Bell, *Faces at the Bottom of the Well: The Permanence of Racism* (Basic Books, 1992); Andrew Hacker, *Two Nations: Black and White, Separate, Hostile, Unequal* (Scribner, 1992).

five   **Affirmative Action**

Orlando Patterson

Affirmative action poses two sets of issues. One has to do with the rationale for, as well as the costs and benefits of, the program itself. The other concerns the extraordinary public debate surrounding it. Normally, public debate of an important policy does not itself become the object of scrutiny, but when that debate is out of all proportion to the issues involved, the forces accounting for the intensity of the debate become a proper subject of inquiry. I suggest that this is one of those cases. As such, affirmative action belongs to a category of public debate that Lee Rainwater and William Yancey once called the politics of controversy.[1]

Affirmative Action and the Politics of Controversy

It is repeatedly asserted that affirmative action comes at great political costs because it is seen as unfair by the overwhelming majority of Americans. Many supporters of affirmative action, accepting the validity of polling data purporting to substantiate this claim, argue that hostility to such efforts has its source in either lingering old-fashioned racism or more sophisticated, modern, symbolic racism. Paul Sniderman and his associates attempt to show that while racism does not inform opposition to affirmative action, "race has become divisive in a new way" by splitting the liberal democratic coalition. Liberals, they find, are deeply divided on principle over the program but are also unable to abandon it for political and principled reasons.[2]

While I am inclined to agree with Sniderman and his colleagues that opposition to affirmative action is not, on the whole, driven by racial prejudice and that it has been a divisive issue for liberals, I think this entire approach is of relevance only in accounting for the politics of controversy surrounding the program. As a way of getting at the truth about Americans' views on affirmative action it is irrelevant because overwhelming support can be shown to exist for the actual affirmative action programs that people have experienced. There is a profound difference between Americans' responses to survey questions about preferences in the abstract and their responses to the actual programs they know about. The first is a questionable exercise in which it is never clear just what it is that the respondents are actually responding to, whereas the meaning is absolutely clear in the second case, because respondents are being asked to state their views about their own experiences with a known program.

What follows in this section is based on my analyses of data drawn from *The General Social Survey Database, 1990,* by the National Opinion Research Center (NORC) of the University of Chicago and from the findings of a Harris poll conducted in 1995.

In 1990 respondents to the NORC survey were asked, "What do you think the chances are these days that a white person won't get a job or promotion while an equally or less qualified Afro-American person gets one instead? Is this very likely, somewhat likely, or not very likely to happen these days?" The question was followed with probes into the reasons respondents held the views they did: Was it "something that happened to you personally?" "something that happened to a relative, family member, or close friend?" something they "saw occurring at work" or "heard about in the media?" and so on.

In response to the speculative question, more than 70 percent of Euro-Americans asserted that other Euro-Americans were being hurt by affirmative action; but when the same group was asked not to speculate about other Euro-Americans but to reflect on their own experiences with the program, only 7 percent claimed to have been influenced by affirmative action. Fewer than one in four had heard about or witnessed anything negative concerning affirmative action at their workplace. When a NORC poll four years later asked respondents what they themselves thought about preferences in general, again the overwhelming majority of Euro-Americans were opposed. Indeed, half of all Afro-American men opposed hypothetical preferences, a reaction that alone should raise questions about just what respondents imagined they were responding to.

The contrast is remarkable. When Americans speculate in the abstract about the ethics of preferential scenarios, they oppose affirmative action. When they think about the real, concrete, affirmative action programs they know about and experience at their workplace, they support it. A Harris poll in June 1995 confirmed that support: 80 percent of Americans polled thought that their employers were doing just about the right amount, or not enough, for women and minorities. Commenting on the remarkable difference between these results and those frequently cited by opponents of affirmative action, Humphrey Taylor, the CEO of the Harris polling firm, wrote, "There is a world of difference between people's general attitudes to such programs and their actual experiences with their own employers' policies."[3]

When Americans are asked what they think about affirmative action in the abstract, they merely relay what they have read or heard in the media. The 1994 NORC poll specifically asked respondents where they had received their negative views about the program and found that the single most important source of information was the media, mentioned by 42 percent of Euro-Americans. The result has been a self-confirming media distortion of Americans' views on the subject. The media, having declared the subject controversial and divisive, then conduct polls asking respondents if the program is controversial and divisive. Respondents tell the media pollsters what they want to hear, based on what they have recently heard or read in the media. The media then reports these results as further proof that the program is highly divisive, confirming the opinions it initiated and at the same time beginning a new cycle in the escalating process of self-confirming disparagement of the program.

Even more disturbing is the media's failure to report that the overwhelming majority of American workers and managers strongly supports the affirmative action programs at their workplaces. The media is by no means a disinterested player in this matter. Affirmative action programs at the nation's media organizations have been greatly resented by many established journalists—the very people who make critical decisions about what to highlight or neglect in news reports. The important 1995 Harris poll, for example, received almost no notice from the media. The later survey, according to Taylor, "shows that the media have greatly overplayed the myth of the Euro-American male backlash and failed to report that the overwhelming majority of workers feel they have been treated fairly in the workplace. *This is yet another case of a small, vocal minority being perceived as a majority.*"[4]

Political opponents of affirmative action, being fully aware of the discrepancy between opposition to preferences posed in the abstract and support of actual affirmative action programs they know about, exploit it by carefully avoiding any wording that mentions affirmative action in their own campaigns against the program. Indeed, in the campaign to repeal affirmative action in California, the petition against the program went to great and successful lengths to avoid any reference to the term *affirmative action* in the wording that finally appeared on the ballot. There is now reason to believe that a significant minority of those who voted for the petition did so thinking that they were voting on behalf of affirmative action and that this group was large enough to have defeated the petition had they voted for what they thought they were voting for. California's Proposition 209 may well have been a subversion of the democratic process.

One of the great political ironies of affirmative action, brilliantly documented by John Skrentny in a major study of the historical sociology of the policy, is the fact that its most radical phase was put in place by none other than President Richard Nixon, as the Machiavellian centerpiece of his "wedge" strategy to drive Euro-Americans in the South from the Democratic party and to split the coalition of liberal Euro-Americans and disadvantaged minorities, especially Afro-Americans, that emerged with the civil rights movement.[5]

On both counts the strategy was a great success. Southern Euro-Americans made an epochal political shift to the Republican party. Long after Nixon departed in disgrace from the presidency, affirmative action continued to be used as an effective wedge tool by conservative Republicans in trouble, the most notorious case being that of Jesse Helms in his nearly losing struggle to retain his Senate seat against a moderate Afro-American contender. At the same time, formerly liberal northern Euro-Americans abandoned the civil rights coalition for the movement known as neoconservatism.

Not all opponents of affirmative action are politically or personally motivated, however. The vocal minority opposed to it consists not only of liberals but also moderate conservatives and even some on the left who, while remaining sympathetic to the plight of disadvantaged minorities, are nonetheless troubled, for the most principled of reasons, by many aspects of affirmative action. These are the people whose views have been eloquently discussed by Sniderman and his associates. The issues they raise about the moral, social, and economic costs of the policy are real and must be taken seriously by all who continue to defend affirmative action, however shocked they may be by those who cynically use it as a racially divisive wedge strategy and then claim that it has racially divided the nation.

I have previously addressed some of the more important moral and social objections raised by thoughtful and sympathetic critics of affirmative action elsewhere.[6] In the remainder of this chapter, I outline a sociological argument for the necessity of affirmative action and its continuation for another fifteen years or so.

The Liability of Isolation

In the workplace, as in many aspects of their lives, Afro-Americans as a group are systematically unconnected to the essential network resources that most other Americans take for granted. Their workplace isolation involves far more than the impenetrable "glass ceilings" associated with the nation's boardrooms. It is pervasive, hampering working-class laborers seeking well-paying jobs on a construction work crew just as it does upwardly mobile college graduates. This isolation can be addressed, but only partially, by access to improved educational opportunities. Such opportunities might compensate for network deficiencies in the long run, mainly through introducing Afro-American students to other students with wider network ranges, but the process is painfully slow. For a group as unconnected as Afro-Americans, it may take multiple generations. Speeding up this process requires affirmative action.

The fundamental insight of network sociologists is that people's ties to others structure the flow of information that both socializes them as they grow up and provide them with the social resources critical for competent functioning as adults. Economic behavior in particular, as noted by Mark Granovetter in his 1974 book *Getting a Job*, is "heavily embedded in other social processes that closely constrain and determine its course and results."[7] Without denying the importance of individual attributes in accounting for success, network sociologists nevertheless consider past and present structures of network ties and their attendant information flows to be of at least equal importance in explaining a person's achievements. As sociologists Nan Lin, Walter Ensel, and John Vaughn explain, the network approach "challenges the assumption that the labor market is essentially an open and competitive arena where specifications for a job and the necessary skills and competence are easily matched and where information about job and applicant availability is widely diffused."[8]

Karen Campbell, Peter Marsden, and Jeanne Hurlbert demonstrate that networks operate as crucial resources for individuals in three ways. First, networks help individuals find a job, a home, or even a spouse. Second, they provide access to influential people. Finally, they promote bargaining skills that enlarge the range and influence of networks even more.[9] As Granovetter notes, "careers are not made up of random jumps from one job to another, but rather . . . individuals rely on contacts acquired at various stages of their work-life and before. One important result of this is that mobility appears to be self-generating: the more different social and work settings one moves through, the larger the reservoir of personal contacts he has who may mediate further mobility."[10]

No ethnic group has ever achieved success in America by relying solely on education. Instead, immigrants—even ethnic groups that have powerful religious and social sanctions against such interethnic bonding—have made inroads into established American networks. Welcomed to the neighborhoods, clubs, and churches of existing groups, newcomers have developed ties that extend their network ranges, especially in job searches and in getting credit for mortgages and small businesses.

Ethnic intermarriages have also contributed to Euro-American immigrants' success, both by extending their range of network ties and by involving them in new dense networks of strong affinal ties. Intermarriage enhances network bargaining skills in two ways: it encourages creative thinking about networking (imagine a Jewish groom's first Sunday dinner with his Italian wife's family), and it teaches traditions of network bargaining peculiar to the spouse's ethnic group. More broadly, intermarriage encourages cultural and intellectual innovation. The explosive growth of artistic, scientific, technical, and entrepreneurial innovations in the United States is certainly linked to the high rate of intermarriage among its ethnic groups.

Afro-Americans, however, have been almost completely isolated from this national process. They are, for example, residentially isolated (see tables 5-1 and 5-2). Douglas Massey and Nancy Denton note that the data in table 5-1

reveal the full extent of black racial seclusion within U.S. metropolitan areas, both northern and southern. The average value changed little over the decade and remained close to 66% in both regions; and in 1980 no metropolitan area displayed an isolation index under 50%. Despite the legal banning of discrimination and the apparent easing of white racial hostility, blacks and whites were still very unlikely to share a neighborhood within most metropolitan areas. In many cases, the degree of black spatial isolation was extreme.[11]

There are, to be sure, some positive signs. Table 5-2 indicates modest recent improvement in some cities, and a surprising level of interracial contact, mainly originating at work, has been reported in polls despite continued spatial segregation. Even so, it is astonishing that, after living almost three centuries in this country, Afro-Americans have remained so spatially isolated.

Partly related to the group's spatial segregation is its marital isolation. The intermarriage rates of Afro-Americans with non-Afro-Amer-

Table 5-1. Trends in Black Segregation, Selected Metropolitan Areas with Large Black Populations, 1970 and 1980[a]

Percent

Metropolitan area	Black-white segregation		Black isolation	
	1970	1980	1970	1980
North				
Boston	82	78	57	55
Chicago	92	88	86	83
Detroit	88	87	76	77
Los Angeles	91	81	70	60
New York	81	82	59	63
Philadelphia	80	79	68	70
South				
Atlanta	82	79	78	75
Birmingham	38	41	45	50
Dallas	87	77	76	64
Memphis	76	72	78	76
Miami	85	78	75	64
Washington	81	70	77	68

Source: Douglas S. Massey and Nancy A. Denton, *American Apartheid: Segregation and the Making of the Underclass* (Harvard, 1993).

a. Black-white segregation is measured by an index of dissimilarity, which gives the percentage of Afro-Americans who would have to move to achieve an "even" residential pattern—one in which every neighborhood replicates the racial composition of the city. Black isolation is measured by an index that measures the degree to which Afro-Americans reside in neighborhoods that are mainly Afro-American: the index is 100 when all Afro-Americans live in exclusively Afro-American neighborhoods; it is less than fifty when they live in neighborhoods that are more Euro-American than Afro-American.

icans are far lower than those of other ethnic groups. Researchers often express the extent of intermarriage in terms of the proportion of women in a given group who marry men from other groups, but that measure is misleading because it fails to take account of compositional factors such as the relative sizes of the groups involved. A much better approach, that taken by Stanley Lieberson and Mary Waters, is to measure intermarriage in terms of the rate that would be expected if spouses were chosen randomly in the population.[12] I have calculated this rate using 1990 census data.

The data in table 5-3 indicate that Afro-American women have by far the highest in-marriage rate of all ethnic groups, but this figure grossly underestimates the true level of isolation by not taking account of the proportion of all Americans who are Afro-American. The proportion of husbands of each ethnic group in the population as a whole is the

Table 5-2. Trends in Black Segregation, Selected Metropolitan Areas, 1980 and 1990

Percent

Metropolitan area	Black-white segregation, 1980	Metropolitan area	Black-white segregation, 1990
	Most segregated		
Bradenton, Fla.	91	Gary, Ind.	91
Chicago	91	Detroit	89
Gary, Ind.	90	Chicago	87
Sarasota, Fla.	90	Cleveland	86
Cleveland	89	Buffalo, N.Y.	84
Detroit	89	Flint, Mich.	84
	Least segregated		
Fayetteville, N.C.	43	Clarksville, Tenn.	42
Lawton, Okla.	43	Lawrence, Kans.	41
Anchorage, Alaska	42	Fayetteville, N.C.	41
Danville, Va.	41	Anchorage, Alaska	38
Lawrence, Kans.	38	Lawton, Okla.	37
Jacksonville, N.C.	36	Jacksonville, N.C.	31

Source: Reynolds Farley and William H. Frey, "Changes in the Segregation of Whites from Blacks during the 1980s: Small Steps toward a More Integrated Society," *American Sociological Review* 49 (1994), pp. 23–45.

proportion of such husbands we would expect to find in each ethnic group under conditions of random marital choice. The proportion of Afro-American husbands in the population as a whole, 5.1 percent, is what the in-marriage rate of Afro-American women would be if marital choices were random. The ratio of in-marriages to out-marriages for Afro-American women is 82.3; thus we begin to see the true extent of Afro-American marital isolation.

The ratio of husbands within each group to husbands outside the group for all women outside the group indicates that the ratio of Afro-American husbands to non-Afro-American husbands for all non-Afro-American women is 0.003; the odds ratio derived from the ratios of Afro-American to non-Afro-American women's marital choices—the best measure of Afro-American marital isolation—tells us that the odds that an Afro-American woman will marry an Afro-American man are 27,444 times greater than that a non-Afro-American woman will marry an Afro-American man! Compare this ratio with the odds ratios of other ethnic groups.

Table 5-3. Intermarriage Rates, American-Born Women in Their First Marriages, 1990

Group	Women, in-married (%)	All husbands (%)	In-out ratio Group	In-out ratio Others	Odds ratio
English-American	60.7	11.5	1.544	0.097	15.910
German-American	68.0	22.5	2.125	0.219	9.700
Irish-American	53.1	10.1	1.132	0.092	12.185
French-American	41.2	2.6	0.700	0.025	28.000
Italian-American	54.5	4.6	1.197	0.041	29.190
Polish-American	49.8	2.8	0.992	0.024	41.330
Swedish-American	40.5	1.4	0.680	0.014	48.500
Afro-American	98.8	5.1	82.330	0.003	27,444.000
Mexican-American	83.1	1.8	4.917	0.005	983.400
Puerto Rican–American	84.7	0.4	5.535	0.002	2,767.500

Source: Orlando Patterson, *Rituals of Blood: Consequences of Slavery in Two American Centuries* (Washington, D.C.: Civitas, 1998), p. 157.

Further evidence on Afro-American isolation comes from sociological studies of American's core networks: those people with whom they discuss "important matters." The NORC *General Social Survey Database, 1985* (the first nationwide sample of core network data) found striking racial and ethnic homogeneity in these networks. (The enormous liability of Afro-American marital isolation becomes even clearer when we learn that the typical American core network is small and centered on kin.) Significant variations, however, exist across subgroups. Not surprisingly, whites have the largest networks, Afro-Americans the smallest. One troubling finding of this and other studies is that, contrary to the identity rhetoric of Afro-American leaders and the claims of many sociologists, Afro-Americans do not compensate for their isolation from other groups by relying more heavily on kinsmen. To the contrary, as Peter Marsden, a preeminent network scholar, notes, "black respondents cited fewer kin and fewer non-kin than whites did, and their networks have a lower proportion of kin than those of whites."[13]

Enter Affirmative Action

Affirmative action can best be seen as a medium-term strategy to supplement and expedite the long-term educational solution to the unfair isolation of Afro-Americans. It directly addresses and compensates for their network liability by inserting them into the network-rich educational institutions of the nation and the self-generating career networks at the workplace—networks that Euro-Americans take for granted.

Affirmative action in the educational sector builds networks in several ways. First, it helps youngsters gain skills. Defenders of affirmative action usually emphasize this role, but such a strategy cannot justify why students from disadvantaged backgrounds should be at the nation's elite colleges if adequate educational alternatives exist for them that are congruent with their educational records. Indeed, as a bigger fish in a smaller pond, a talented Afro-American student may well acquire more purely technical skills at a good state institution than at Harvard.

Although educators are loath to admit it, elite educational institutions serve two primary functions: to recruit and educate the nation's elite and to provide an environment in which students initiate and extend elite networks and learn network negotiating skills. Living and learning with students from elite environments helps establish wide-ranging links with elite networks as well as dense links through intermarriages.

Given what we now know about the true nature of labor markets, it should be clear that only some form of affirmative action could have inserted Afro-Americans into working-class and middle-class jobs on a significant scale. Economists often express bewilderment at the failure of Afro-Americans' qualifications to match up with their earnings. That a Euro-American construction worker with a high school degree earns more than the typical Afro-American college graduate must be a source of endless disciplinary frustration for those who believe that the price system should match up workers of equal qualifications with jobs paying equal wages. As readers of this chapter know, however, there is an answer to this puzzle: networks.

Mark Granovetter's description of the utility of networks in *Getting a Job* provides an excellent rationale for affirmative action intervention in the labor market:

> Especially important to recognize, moreover, is the self-maintaining aspect of personal contact systems. Blacks are at a disadvantage in using channels of job information not because they have failed

to "develop an informal structure" suitable to the need, but because they are presently under-represented in the structure of employment itself. If those presently employed in a given industry or firm have no black friends, no blacks will enter those settings through personal contacts. Once a core of blacks (or whatever group in question) has become established, however, a multiplier effect can be anticipated, as they recruit friends and relatives, who do the same, and so on. Once achieved, this situation is self-sustaining.[14]

Since Granovetter wrote this in 1974, a great deal has been achieved, thanks in good part to precisely this effect of affirmative action. In fact, Granovetter offers not only a rationale for affirmative action but a way of judging where and when it has fulfilled its purpose. Affirmative action can and perhaps should be discontinued in any firm that has achieved this self-sustaining recruitment process for minority workers. The self-sustaining group need not coincide with the proportion of the disadvantaged group in the population at large.

Another important area of economic justice that can be remedied only by affirmative action pertains to the role of networks in the internal and external structures of organizations, particularly in middle- and upper-level employment decisions. Organizations, including business firms, rely heavily on informal networks both for the internal structuring of information and decisionmaking and for links with related organizations. At all levels there is not only a tacit culture at play—knowledge of how things really work as distinct from what the job descriptions and work manuals say—but vital network contacts to be made and important network negotiating skills to be learned if one is effectively to mobilize critical network figures and links within and between organizations. Minorities and women are often unconnected to such knowledge and links and may never stand a chance of acquiring them, because they are made, nurtured, and extended precisely in those places where disadvantaged minorities and women are not to be found.

This problem is commonly mentioned, so there is no need to belabor it except to note one important point. The higher up a hierarchy one goes, the more important network factors become in recruitment decisions. An unprejudiced personnel officer bound by a color- or gender-blind code but alert to the organizational need for persons with the right network skills will always be obliged to reject applicants from backgrounds with impoverished network resources. The costs are simply too high to train such people. Where then are these skills to be acquired? They can come only from organizations being pressured or provided with governmental incentives to train people in these skills until a critical mass of them exists.

The Costs and Responsibilities of Affirmative Action

All social policies incur costs, and affirmative action is no exception. The costs to individual Euro-Americans have been so thoroughly discussed that there is no need to repeat them here. One way to minimize the costs is to recognize three basic principles emerging from court decisions as identified by Jim Newman.[15] The first is that the right to retain one's job is sacrosanct and cannot be interfered with by affirmative action under any circumstances. The program is best used in recruiting new workers. Thus one may hire an equally qualified Afro-American teacher over a Euro-American teacher on affirmative action grounds but may not fire a Euro-American teacher instead of an Afro-American one for this reason. Second, while affirmative action is still needed in promotion decisions, ethnic or gender considerations can come into play only when candidates are otherwise equally qualified. Finally, quotas of any kind are prohibited.

Another important consideration concerns the nature of jobs. It might be helpful, for example, to distinguish between knowledge-intensive and network-intensive jobs. A network-intensive job is one for which employers depend heavily on informal contacts when filling vacancies; it also requires a great deal of network negotiating skill for its performance. A knowledge-intensive job is one in which purely technical or cognitive qualifications dominate the recruitment and performance processes. Now, barring sinecures in city halls and family firms around the country, nearly all jobs that are network-intensive also require a minimum level of skills. Many jobs, however, are almost wholly knowledge-intensive. I propose that affirmative action programs exclude such jobs and focus on network-intensive jobs—precisely those that can never be attained through schooling alone. These jobs, incidentally, are to be found at all levels of the occupational hierarchy.

The costs and responsibilities must be borne by the beneficiaries of affirmative action. One danger is that affirmative action may reduce the incentive for beneficiaries to perform at their very best. This troublesome possibility is suggested, for example, by the tendency for Afro-American students to perform below the level predicted by their test scores. I do not know whether the same problem exists at the workplace. One way of addressing or preventing an underachievement problem is for teachers and supervisors to evaluate with scrupulous honesty. Colleges should return to blind grading, and rules should be enacted that forbid all students from revealing their ethnic identities in their examination answers and papers.

The greatest risk of affirmative action is that it might become an institutionalized entitlement program. I strongly suspect that many otherwise sympathetic persons oppose it for precisely this reason. It is not an unreasonable apprehension, given the chronic propensity of government programs to become permanent. I return to this in my final suggestion.

A related, and equally disturbing, danger is that some Afro-American leaders may conspire with segregationist Euro-Americans to stand affirmative action on its head. As this chapter makes clear, the main justification for affirmative action is that it compensates for the liability of isolation of Afro-Americans. It is both a medium-term substitution for, and a jump-start promotion of, the long-term solution of full ethnic integration. As integration is achieved, the need for affirmative action should be lessened. In this way, the program becomes self-canceling.

Two developments, however, hint at a possible subversion of this integrative process. One is the Afro-American identity movement, with its explicit rejection of integration and its celebration of ethnic separatism, as in the tendency of minority students to segregate themselves on the nation's campuses and the increasing propensity for voluntarily segregated neighborhoods among the Afro-American middle class. The other development is best exemplified by the Atlanta model of ethnic relations. This city, which prides itself on being "too busy to hate," has fully embraced affirmative action, creating an environment with which the elites of both groups seem very comfortable. The only problem is that

Atlanta remains extremely segregated. It seems as if a quid pro quo has emerged between the two dominant ethnic groups in which permanent affirmative action is accepted by the Euro-American elite as the price to be paid for the permanent segregation of the two groups, an adaptation of the old southern racist principle: separate, but now truly equal, at least among the elites. Were this indeed the case—and it is merely one interpretation of what is happening in Atlanta—it would be a disastrous contradiction not only of the ends of affirmative action but of its main justification, at least as I argue it.

One way of preventing or aborting such an outcome is to place a time limit on affirmative action. The program has already achieved a great deal, even though Afro-Americans remain badly unconnected and in need of help in overcoming their isolation. I propose that affirmative action be gradually phased out over fifteen years, at which time it would be converted to a class-based program, partly along the lines proposed by Richard D. Kahlenberg.[16] During this period every effort should be made to break down all remaining barriers to integration, including Afro-American resistance to integrated neighborhoods, intermarriage, and transethnic child adoption.

We could begin immediately to reduce the social cost of the program by removing all categories of disadvantaged persons except Afro-Americans, Puerto Ricans, second-generation Mexican Americans and African ancestry persons, Native Americans, and Euro-American women. In another five years or so we should remove all upper-middle-class persons, say those from families with incomes greater than $75,000. Ten years from now only working- and lower-class disadvantaged persons should be eligible, and Euro-American underprivileged persons could be phased in. In fifteen years all ethnic criteria should be dropped; the resulting class-based program should last as long as poverty and underprivileged classes exist. As we ease out of the existing program and shift toward one based on socioeconomic disabilities, it becomes imperative that we reinforce and vigorously enforce laws against discrimination.

Placing a time limit on affirmative action would in all likelihood blunt the orchestrated politics of controversy that now bedevils it. Thinking about phasing it into a class-based entitlement program may at long last bring Americans around to a consideration of the growing inequality that threatens the harmony of our democracy far more than the alarmist cry of racial division.

Notes

1. Lee Rainwater and William L. Yancey, *The Moynihan Report and the Politics of Controversy* (MIT Press, 1967).

2. David O. Sears, "Symbolic Racism," in *Eliminating Racism*, edited by Phyllis Katz and Dalmas Taylor (Plenum Press, 1988); Paul Sniderman and Thomas Piazza, *The Scar of Race* (Harvard University Press, 1993), introduction, chapters 3, 4; Paul Sniderman and Edward Carmines, *Reaching Beyond Race* (Harvard University Press, 1997).

3. Humphrey Taylor, "The Euro-American Backlash, If It Exists, Is Not Based on Personal Experience in the Workplace," *Louis Harris and Associates, Harris Poll*, no. 44 (1995).

4. Ibid.

5. John David Skrentny, *The Ironies of Affirmative Action: Politics, Culture, and Justice in America* (University of Chicago Press, 1996), chapter 7.

6. Orlando Patterson, *The Ordeal of Integration: Progress and Resentment in America's "Racial" Crisis* (Washington, D.C.: Civitas, 1997), chapters 3, 5.

7. Mark Granovetter, *Getting a Job: A Study of Contacts and Careers* (Harvard University Press, 1974), p. 39.

8. Nan Lin, Walter Ensel, and John Vaughn, "Social Resources and Strength of Ties: Structural Factors in Occupational Status Attainment," *American Sociological Review* 46 (1981), pp. 393–405.

9. Karen Campbell, Peter Marsden and Jeanne S. Hurlbert, "Social Resources and Socioeconomic Status," *Social Networks* 8 (1986), pp. 97–117.

10. Granovetter, *Getting a Job*, p. 85;

11. Douglas Massey and Nancy Denton, *American Apartheid: Segregation and the Making of the Underclass* (Harvard University Press, 1993), pp. 65–66.

12. Stanley Lieberson and Mary G. Waters, *From Many Strands: Ethnic and Racial Groups in Contemporary America* (New York: Russell Sage Foundation, 1988).

13. Peter Marsden, "Core Discussion Networks of Americans," *American Sociological Review* 52 (1987), p. 129. See my reanalysis of this data in Orlando Patterson, *Rituals of Blood: Consequences of Slavery in Two American Centuries* (Washington, D.C.: Civitas, 1998), pp. 152–54.

14. Granovetter, *Getting a Job*, p. 133.

15. Jim D. Newman, "Affirmative Action and the Courts," in *Affirmative Action in Perspective*, edited by F. A. Blanchard and F. J. Crosby (Springer-Verlag, 1989), pp. 44–46.

16. Richard D. Kahlenberg, *The Remedy: Class, Race, and Affirmative Action* (Basic Books, 1997).

part three

Education

six

The Black-White Test Score Gap

Christopher Jencks
Meredith Phillips

African Americans score lower than European Americans on vocabulary, reading, and math tests as well as on tests that claim to measure scholastic aptitude and intelligence. The gap appears before children enter kindergarten, and it persists into adulthood. It has narrowed since 1970, but the typical American black still scores below 75 percent of American whites on almost every standardized test. This statistic does not imply, of course, that all blacks score below all whites. There is a lot of overlap between the two groups. Nonetheless, the test score gap is large enough to have important social and economic consequences.

Closing the black-white test score gap would probably do more to promote racial equality in the United States than any other strategy now under serious consideration. Eliminating the test score gap would sharply increase black college graduation rates. It would also reduce racial disparities in men's earnings and would probably eliminate racial disparities in women's earnings. Eliminating the test score gap would also allow selective colleges, professional schools, and employers to phase out the racial preferences that have caused so much political trouble over the past generation. Narrowing the test score gap would require continuous effort by both blacks and whites, and it would probably take more than one generation. But we think it can be done. This conviction rests mainly on three facts.

First, the black-white test score gap has narrowed since the early 1970s. The best trend data come from the National Assessment of Educational Progress (NAEP), which has been testing seventeen-year-olds since 1971.[1] From 1971 to 1996, the black-white reading gap narrowed by almost half and the math gap by a third. According to a study by two sociologists, Min-Hsiung Huang and Robert Hauser, the black-white vocabulary gap also shrank by half among adults born between 1909 and 1969.[2]

Second, even nonverbal IQ scores are sensitive to environmental change. Scores on nonverbal IQ tests have risen dramatically throughout the world since the 1930s. The average American white scored higher on the Stanford-Binet in 1978 than 82 percent of whites who took the test in 1932.

Third, when black or mixed-race children are raised in white rather than black homes, their preadolescent test scores rise dramatically. These adoptees' scores seem to fall during adolescence, but this could easily be because their social and cultural environment comes to resemble that of other black teenagers.

Explaining the Gap

Traditional explanations for the black-white test score gap have not withstood the test of time. During the 1960s, most liberals blamed the gap on the combined effects of black poverty, segregation, and inadequate funding of black schools. Since then, the number of affluent black families has grown dramatically, but their children's test scores still lag far behind those of white children from equally affluent families. Most southern schools desegregated in the early 1970s, and southern black nine-year-olds' reading scores seem to have risen as a result. Even today, black third graders in predominantly white schools read a little better than initially similar blacks who attend predominantly black schools. Large racial differences in reading skills persist, however, even in desegregated schools, and a school's racial mix has little effect on reading scores after sixth grade or on math scores at any age.

Despite glaring economic inequalities between a few rich suburbs and nearby central cities, the average black child and average white child now live in school districts that spend almost exactly the same amount per pupil. Black and white schools also have about the same number of teachers per pupil, about the same pay scales, and teachers with almost the same amount of formal education and teaching experience. The most important resource difference between black and white schools seems to be that both black and white teachers in black schools have lower test scores than their counterparts in white schools.

From an empirical standpoint, traditional conservative explanations for the gap—genes, a culture of poverty, and single motherhood—are no more persuasive than their liberal counterparts. Scientists have identified only a handful of the genes that affect test performance, so we have no direct genetic evidence regarding innate cognitive differences between blacks and whites. We have, however, accumulated a fair amount of indirect evidence since 1970. Most of it suggests that whether children live in a black or white environment has far more impact on their test performance than the number of Africans or Europeans in their family tree. While cultural differences associated with chronic poverty may account for some of the black-white test score gap, the culture of poverty cannot be the main explanation, because a large test score gap persists even among affluent children. And while children raised by single mothers score lower on most standardized tests than children raised by married couples, this difference almost disappears once we take account of the fact that women who become single mothers come from less advantaged families, have lower test scores, and complete less schooling than women with husbands.

New Directions

We suspect that successful new explanations for the test score gap will differ from their predecessors in at least three ways.

First, instead of looking mainly for resource differences between predominantly black and predominantly white schools, successful theories will probably concentrate on differences in the way black and white schools spend the resources available to them. For example, predominantly black schools enroll far more children with severe academic and behavioral problems than white schools do. Such children consume more resources than the average child, which in turn prevents ordinary black children from getting as much attention and support as their counterparts in white schools.

Second, instead of concentrating on whether teachers treat black and white children differently, successful theories will probably pay more attention to the way black and white children respond to the same classroom experiences, such as having a teacher of a different race or having a teacher with low expectations for students who read below their grade level.

Third, instead of emphasizing families' economic and educational resources, successful theories will pay more attention to the way family members and friends interact with one another and with the outside world. A good explanation of why white four-year-olds have bigger vocabularies than black four-year-olds is likely to focus on how much the parents talk to their children, how they deal with their children's questions, and how they react when their children either learn or fail to learn something, not on how much money the parents have in the bank.

Psychological and cultural differences are hard to describe accurately and therefore easy to exaggerate. Collecting accurate data on such differences would probably require an investment of time and effort comparable to what went into developing cognitive tests during the first half of the twentieth century. It would also require far closer cooperation between psychologists, ethnographers, and survey researchers than one ordinarily sees in academic life.

Policy Implications

Our argument that reducing the black-white test score gap would do more to move America toward racial equality than any politically plausible alternative rests on two problematic premises: that policies aimed at reducing the test score gap are in fact politically feasible and that such policies can in fact reduce the gap.

Public support for almost any policy depends partly on whether the beneficiaries are perceived as deserving or undeserving. One obvious advantage of programs directed at children is that hardly anyone blames first graders' ignorance on their lack of motivation. First graders of every race seem eager to please. Both black and white adults often think that older black children lack academic motivation, but most adults still blame this on the children's parents or schools, not on the children themselves. That was why Lyndon Johnson placed so much emphasis on helping children in his original war on poverty program.

Policies that reduce the black-white gap will not, of course, be politically popular if they improve black children's scores at white children's expense. Both school desegregation and the elimination of academically selective classes in desegregated schools have aroused strong white resistance because of the perceived cost to white children. But these two policies would not do blacks much good even if whites were willing to adopt them. The most promising school-related strategies for reducing the black-white test score gap involve changes like reducing class size, setting minimum standards of academic competency for teachers, and raising teachers' expectations for low-performing students. All these changes would benefit both blacks and whites, but all appear to be especially beneficial to blacks.

The results from the Tennessee class size experiment indicate, for example, that cutting class size in the early grades raises both black and white children's test scores but raises black children's scores more. Historical evidence also seems to support the hypothesis that lowering class size helps narrow the black-white test score gap. When low birth rates reduced school enrollment in the 1970s, the teacher-pupil ratio rose and classes shrank. Independent analyses by Ronald Ferguson and David Grissmer suggest that this class size reduction was followed by a marked decline in the black-white test score gap.[3]

Although measuring teachers' competence is harder than counting the number of children in a classroom, teachers' test scores show a stronger association than any other widely used measure of teacher quality with how much students learn. Screening teachers for verbal and mathematical competence is thus likely to boost children's performance. Since the teachers who fail competency tests are concentrated in black schools, such exams would probably prove especially beneficial to black students, although this benefit may be partially offset by the fact that the teachers who fail such tests are also disproportionately black.

Ferguson's review of the literature on teachers' expectations concludes that teachers do have lower expectations for blacks than for whites but that this is largely because blacks enter school with weaker cognitive skills than whites and learn a bit less after entering.[4] Ferguson also finds some evidence that low teacher expectations have a more negative effect on black children than on their white classmates.

Although we believe that improving the nation's schools would help reduce the black-white test score gap, schools alone cannot eliminate the gap. The typical black four-year-old's vocabulary score falls below the twentieth percentile of the national distribution. Relying entirely on educational reform to move such a child up to the fiftieth percentile does not strike us as realistic. If we want equal outcomes among twelfth graders, we will have to narrow the skill gap between black and white children before they enter school. There are two ways to do this: change black children's preschool experiences and change their home experiences.

A review of research on preschool effects by Steven Barnett, a professor of education at Rutgers, strongly suggests that cognitively oriented preschool programs can improve black children's achievement scores, even though the benefits fade somewhat as children age.[5] Unfortunately, black preschoolers are concentrated in Head Start centers, which do not currently emphasize cognitive development. Changing this emphasis should be a high priority.

Parenting practices almost certainly have more impact on children's cognitive development than preschool practices, but getting parents to change their habits is even harder than getting teachers to change. Like teachers, parents are usually suspicious of unsolicited advice about how to deal with their children; however, once parents become convinced that a particular practice really helps their children, many adopt it. As a practical political matter, whites cannot tell black parents to change their parenting practices without provoking charges of ethnocentrism, racism, and much else. Further, black parents are hardly the only ones who need help. We should be promoting better parenting practices for *all* parents using every tool at our disposal, from preschool outreach programs and home visits by nurses to television programs and anything else that looks promising.

Finally, a successful strategy for raising black children's test scores depends on convincing both blacks and whites that the gap is not genetic in origin. Genetic variation does explain a substantial fraction of the variation in cognitive skills among people of the same race. So does environmental variation. Once hereditarianism percolates into popular culture, however, it can easily became an excuse for treating academic failure as an inevitable fact of nature. Teaching children skills that do not seem to come naturally is hard work. If our culture allows us to avoid such work by saying that a child simply lacks the required aptitude to master the skills, both teachers and parents will sometimes use this as an excuse for not trying. Blaming failure on lack of ability rather than lack of effort is likely to have especially negative consequences for African American children, who start off behind white children and therefore need to work even harder than white children if they are to catch up.

Time for Renewed Attention

We are convinced that reducing the black-white test score gap is both necessary and possible. We do not have a detailed blueprint for achieving this goal—and neither does anyone else. This is partly because psychologists, sociologists, and educational researchers have devoted far less attention to the test score gap over the past quarter century than its political and social consequences have warranted. Most social scientists have chosen safer topics and hoped the problem would go away. We can do better.

Notes

1. For 1971–94 NAEP data, see Christopher Jencks and Meredith Phillips, eds., *The Black-White Test Score Gap* (Brookings, 1998), p. 4.

2. Min-Hsiung Huang and Robert Hauser, "Trends in Black-White Test Score Differentials: II, The WORDSOM Vocabulary Test," in *The Rising Curve: Long-Term Gains in IQ and Related Measures*, edited by Ulrich Neisser (Washington, D.C.: American Psychological Association, 1998), pp. 303–34.

3. See Jencks and Phillips, *The Black-White Test Score Gap*, pp. 182–226 and pp. 318–74. On the Tennessee experiment, see Frederick Mosteller, "The Tennessee Study of Class Size in the Early Grades," *Future of Children* 5 (Summer-Fall 1995), pp. 113–27.

4. Ronald Ferguson, "Teachers' Perceptions and Expectations and the Black-White Test Score Gap," in Jencks and Phillips, *The Black-White Test Score Gap*, pp. 273–317.

5. Steve Barnett, "Long-Term Effects of Early Childhood Programs on Cognitive and School Outcomes," *Future of Children* 5 (Winter 1995), pp. 25–50.

seven **Race, Education, and Equal Opportunity**

Linda Darling-Hammond

W. E. B. Du Bois was right about the problem of the twenty-first century. The color line divides us still. In recent years, the most visible evidence of this in the public policy arena has been the persistent attack on affirmative action in higher education and employment. From the perspective of the many Americans who believe that the vestiges of discrimination have disappeared, affirmative action now provides an unfair advantage to minorities. From the perspective of those who daily experience the consequences of ongoing discrimination, affirmative action is needed to protect opportunities likely to evaporate if an affirmative obligation to act fairly does not exist. For Americans of all backgrounds, the allocation of opportunity in a society that is becoming ever more dependent on knowledge and education is a source of great anxiety and concern.

At the center of these debates are interpretations of the gaps in educational achievement between white and non-Asian minority students as measured by standardized test scores. The presumption that guides much of the conversation is that equal opportunity now exists; therefore, continued low levels of achievement on the part of minority students must be a function of genes, culture, or a lack of effort and will.[1]

The assumptions that undergird this debate miss an important reality: educational outcomes for minority children are much more a function of their unequal access to key educational resources, including skilled teachers and quality curricula, than they are a function of race. In fact, the U.S. educational system is one of the most unequal in the industrialized world, and students routinely have dramatically different learning opportunities based on their social status. In contrast to European and Asian nations that fund schools centrally and equally, the wealthiest 10 percent of U.S. school districts spend nearly ten times more than the poorest 10 percent, and spending ratios of three to one are common within states. Despite stark differences in funding, teacher quality, curriculum, and class size, the prevailing view is that if students do not achieve, it is their own fault. If we are ever to get beyond the problem of the color line, we must confront and address these inequalities.

The Nature of Educational Inequality

Americans often forget that as late as the 1960s most African American, Latino, and Native American students were educated in wholly segregated schools funded at rates many times lower than those serving whites and that they were excluded from many higher education institutions entirely. The end of legal segregation followed by efforts to equalize spending since 1970 has made a substantial difference in student achievement. On every major national test, including the National Assessment of Educational Progress, the gap in minority and white students' test scores narrowed substantially between 1970 and 1990, especially among elementary school students. On the Scholastic Aptitude Test (SAT), the scores of African American students climbed fifty-four points between 1976 and 1994, while those of white students remained stable.

Even so, educational experiences for minority students have continued to be substantially separate and unequal. Two-thirds of minority students still attend schools that are predominantly minority, most of them located in central cities and funded well below those in neighboring suburban districts. Analyses of data prepared for school finance cases in Alabama, New Jersey, New York, Louisiana, and Texas find that on every tangible measure—from qualified teachers to curricular offerings—schools serving greater numbers of students of color have significantly fewer resources than schools serving mostly white students. As William Taylor and Dianne Piche noted in a report to Congress: "Inequitable systems of school finance inflict disproportionate harm on minority and economically disadvantaged students. Such students are concentrated in states primarily in the South, with the lowest capacities to finance public education. The states with the widest disparities in educational expenditures are large industrial states, in which many minorities and economically disadvantaged students are located in property-poor urban districts which fare the worst in educational expenditures or in rural districts, which suffer from fiscal inequity."[2]

Jonathan Kozol's 1991 *Savage Inequalities* describes the striking differences between public schools serving students of color in urban settings and their suburban counterparts, which typically spend twice as much per student for populations with many fewer special needs.[3] Contrast MacKenzie High School in Detroit, where word processing courses are taught without word processors because the school cannot afford them, or East St. Louis Senior High School, whose biology laboratory has no laboratory tables or usable dissecting kits, with nearby suburban schools, where children enjoy a computer hookup to the Dow Jones to study stock transactions and science laboratories that rival those in some industries. Or contrast Paterson, New Jersey, which could not afford the qualified teachers needed to offer foreign language courses to most high school students, with Princeton, where foreign languages begin in elementary school.

Even within school districts, schools with high concentrations of low-income and minority students receive fewer instructional resources than others. Tracking systems exacerbate these inequalities by segregating many low-income and minority students within schools. In combination, these policies leave minority students with fewer and lower-quality books, curricular materials, laboratories, and computers; significantly larger class sizes; less-qualified and less-experienced teachers; and less access to high-quality curricula. Many schools serving low-income and minority students do not even offer the math and science courses needed for college, and they provide lower-quality teaching in the classes they do offer. It all adds up.

What Difference Does It Make?

Since the 1966 Coleman report, *Equality of Educational Opportunity*, a debate has been waged as to whether money makes a difference to educational outcomes.[4] It is certainly possible to spend money ineffectively; however, studies that have developed sophisticated measures of schooling show that money, properly spent, makes a difference. Four factors consistently influence student achievement, all else equal: students perform better if they are educated in smaller schools where they are well known (three hundred to six hundred students is optimal), have smaller class sizes (especially at the elementary level), have access to challenging curricula, and have more highly qualified teachers.[5]

Minority students are much less likely than white children to have access to these resources. In predominantly minority schools, which most students of color attend, school size averages more than twice that of predominantly white schools and reaches two thousand students or more in most cities; regular class sizes are 80 percent larger on average; curricular offerings and materials are lower in quality; and teachers are much less qualified in terms of education, certification, and training in the fields they teach. In integrated schools, most minority students are segregated in lower-track classes with larger class sizes, less qualified teachers, and lower-quality curricula.[6]

Research shows that teachers' preparation makes a tremendous difference to children's learning. In an analysis of nine hundred Texas school districts, Harvard economist Ronald Ferguson found that teachers' expertise (as measured by scores on a licensing examination, master's degrees, and experience) was the single most important determinant of student achievement, accounting for roughly 40 percent of the measured variance in students' reading and mathematics achievement in grades one through twelve.[7] After controlling for socioeconomic status, the large disparities in achievement between black and white students were almost entirely due to differences in the qualifications of their teachers. In combination, differences in teacher expertise and class size accounted for as much of the measured variance in achievement as did student and family background factors (figure 7-1).

Figure 7-1. Influences on Student Achievement[a]

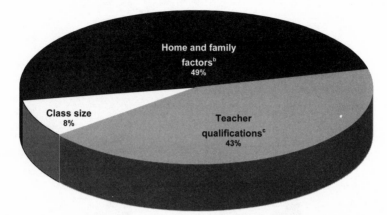

Source: Developed from data in Ronald F. Ferguson, "Paying for Public Education: New Evidence on How and Why Money Matters," *Harvard Journal of Legislation* 28 (Summer 1991), pp. 465–98.
a. Proportion of explained variance in math test score gains, grades three to five.
b. Parent education, income, language background, race, and location.
c. Licensing examination scores, education, and experience.

Ferguson and Duke economist Helen Ladd conducted a similar analysis in Alabama and again found sizable influences of teacher qualifications and smaller class sizes on achievement gains in mathematics and reading. They also found that more of the difference between the high- and low-scoring districts was explained by these two factors than by poverty, race, and parent education.[8] Meanwhile, a Tennessee study found that elementary school students who are assigned to ineffective teachers for three years in a row score nearly fifty percentile points lower on mathematics achievement tests than those assigned to highly effective teachers over the same period.[9] Strikingly, minority students are about half as likely to be assigned to the most effective teachers and nearly twice as likely to be assigned to the least effective.

Minority students are put at greatest risk by the American tradition of allowing enormous variation in the qualifications of teachers. The National Commission on Teaching and America's Future found that new teachers hired without meeting certification standards (25 percent of all new teachers) are usually assigned to teach the most disadvantaged students in low-income and high-minority schools, while the most highly

Figure 7-2. Qualifications of Newly Hired Teachers, by School Type, 1994

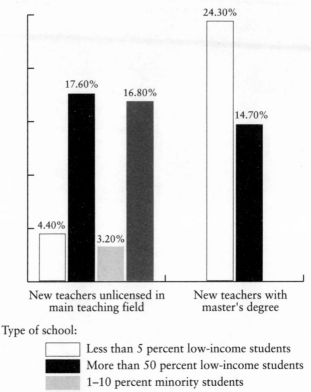

Type of school:

☐ Less than 5 percent low-income students
■ More than 50 percent low-income students
▨ 1–10 percent minority students
■ More than 50 percent minority students

Source: Tabulations of Schools and Staffing Surveys, 1993–94, by the National Commission on Teaching and America's Future, published in Linda Darling-Hammond, *Doing What Matters Most: Investing in Quality Teaching* (New York: National Commission on Teaching and America's Future, 1997).

educated new teachers are hired largely by wealthier schools (figure 7-2).[10] Students in poor or predominantly minority schools are much less likely to have teachers who are fully qualified or who hold degrees higher than the bachelor's. In schools with the highest minority enrollments, for example, students have less than a 50 percent chance of getting a math or science teacher with a license and a degree in the field. In 1994, fully one-third of teachers in high-poverty schools taught without even a minor in their main field, and nearly 70 percent taught without a minor in their secondary teaching field.

Studies of uncertified and underprepared teachers consistently find that they are less effective with students and that they have difficulty with curriculum development, classroom management, student motivation, and teaching strategies. With little knowledge about how children grow, learn, and develop and about what to do to support their learning, these teachers are less likely to understand students' learning styles and differences, to anticipate students' knowledge and potential difficulties, or to plan and redirect instruction to meet students' needs. They are unlikely to see it as their job to do so, often blaming the students if their teaching is not successful.[11]

Teacher expertise and curricular quality are interrelated, because a challenging curriculum requires an expert teacher. Research finds that both students and teachers are tracked: that is, the most expert teachers teach the most demanding courses to the most advantaged students, while lower-track students assigned to less able teachers receive lower quality teaching and less-demanding material. Assignment to tracks is also related to race: even when grades and test scores are comparable, black students are more likely to be assigned to lower-track, nonacademic classes.

When Opportunity Is More Equal

What happens when students of color do get access to more equal opportunities? Studies find that curricular quality and teacher skill make more difference to educational outcomes than students' initial test scores or racial background. Analyses of national data from both the High School and Beyond Surveys and the National Educational Longitudinal Surveys demonstrate that, while there are dramatic differences among students of various racial and ethnic groups in course taking in such areas as math, science, and foreign language, for students with similar course-taking records, achievement test score differences by race or ethnicity narrow substantially.[12]

Robert Dreeben and colleagues at the University of Chicago conducted a long series of studies documenting both the relationship between educational opportunities and student performance and minority students' access to those opportunities.[13] In a comparative study of three hundred Chicago first graders, for example, Dreeben found that African American and white students who had comparable instruction achieved comparable levels of reading skill. He also found that the quality of instruction given African American students was, on average, much lower than that given white students, thus creating a racial gap in aggregate achievement at the end of first grade. In fact, the highest ability group in Dreeben's sample was in a school in a low-income African American neighborhood. These children, though, learned less during first grade than their white counterparts because their teacher was unable to provide the challenging instruction they deserved.

When schools have radically different teaching forces, the effects can be profound. For example, when Eleanor Armour-Thomas and colleagues compared a group of exceptionally effective elementary schools with a group of low-achieving schools with similar demographic characteristics in New York City, roughly 90 percent of the variance in student reading and mathematics scores at grades three, six, and eight was a function of differences in teacher qualifications. The schools with highly qualified teachers serving large numbers of minority and low-income students performed as well as much more advantaged schools.[14]

Most studies estimate effects statistically. However, an experiment that randomly assigned seventh grade "at-risk" students to remedial, average, and honors mathematics classes found that the at-risk students who took the honors class in pre-algebra ultimately outperformed all other students of similar background. Another study compared African American high school youth randomly placed in public housing in the Chicago suburbs with city-placed peers of equivalent income and initial academic attainment and found that the suburban students, who attended largely white and better-funded schools, were substantially more likely to take challenging courses, perform well academically, graduate on time, attend college, and find good jobs.[15]

What Can Be Done?

This state of affairs is not inevitable. The National Commission on Teaching and America's Future issued a blueprint for a comprehensive set of policies to ensure a "caring, competent, and qualified teacher for every child" as well as schools organized to support student success.[16] Fifteen states are working directly with the commission on this agenda, and more than twenty have passed legislation aimed at improving the quality of teaching in all communities. Federal legislation has been proposed by both parties in the past two years to ensure that highly qualified teachers are recruited and prepared to teach students in all schools.[17]

Federal policymakers can develop incentives, as they have in medicine, to guarantee a supply of well-prepared teachers in fields with shortages to teach in high-need locations. States can equalize education spending, enforce higher teaching standards, and reduce teacher shortages, as Connecticut, Kentucky, and North Carolina have already done. Student achievement in these states has climbed as a result.[18] School districts can reallocate resources from administrative superstructures and special add-on programs to support better-educated teachers, who can offer challenging curricula in smaller schools and classes, as restructured schools as far apart as New York and San Diego have done. These schools, in communities where children are normally written off to spend their lives in poverty, welfare dependency, or incarceration, already show much higher levels of achievement for students of color, sending more than 90 percent of their students to college.[19] Focusing on what matters most can make a real difference in what children have the opportunity to learn. This, in turn, makes a difference in what communities can accomplish.

An Entitlement to Good Teaching

The common presumption about educational inequality—that it resides primarily in those students who come to school with inadequate capacities to benefit from what the school has to offer—continues to hold wide currency because the extent of inequality in opportunities to learn is largely unknown. We do not currently operate schools on the presumption that students are entitled to decent teaching and schooling. In fact, some state and local defendants have countered school finance and desegregation cases with assertions that such remedies are not required unless it can be proven that they will produce equal outcomes. Such arguments against equalizing opportunities to learn have made good on Du

Bois's prediction that the problem of the twentieth century would be the problem of the color line.

However, education resources do make a difference, particularly when funds are used to purchase well-qualified teachers and high-quality curricula and to create personalized learning communities in which children are well known. In all of the current Sturm und Drang about affirmative action, special treatment, and the other high-volatility buzzwords for race and class politics in this nation, I offer a simple starting point for the new century's efforts: no special programs, just equal educational opportunity.

Notes

1. See, for example, Richard J. Herrnstein and Charles Murray, *The Bell Curve: Intelligence and Class Structure in American Life* (Free Press, 1994).

2. William L. Taylor and Dianne Piche, *A Report on Shortchanging Children: The Impact of Fiscal Inequity on the Education of Students at Risk*, prepared for the House Committee on Education and Labor (Government Printing Office, 1991).

3. Jonathan Kozol, *Savage Inequalities* (Crown, 1991).

4. James S. Coleman and others, *Equality of Educational Opportunity* (Government Printing Office, 1966).

5. For a review, see Linda Darling-Hammond, *The Right to Learn: A Blueprint for Creating Schools that Work* (San Francisco: Jossey-Bass, 1997).

6. Jeannie Oakes, *Multiplying Inequalities: The Effects of Race, Social Class, and Tracking on Opportunities to Learn Mathematics and Science* (Santa Monica, Calif.: RAND Corporation, 1990); Jeannie Oakes and Martin Lipton, "Tracking and Ability Grouping: A Structural Barrier to Access and Achievement," in *Access to Knowledge: An Agenda for Our Nation's Schools*, edited by John Goodlad and Pamela Keating (New York: College Entrance Examination Board, 1991), pp. 187–204; Gary Orfield, F. Montfort, and M. Aaron, *Status of School Desegregation: 1968–1986* (Alexandria, Va.: National School Boards Association, 1989).

7. Ronald F. Ferguson, "Paying for Public Education: New Evidence on How and Why Money Matters," *Harvard Journal of Legislation* 28 (Summer 1991), pp. 465–98.

8. Ronald F. Ferguson and Helen F. Ladd, "How and Why Money Matters: An Analysis of Alabama Schools," in *Holding Schools Accountable*, edited by Helen F. Ladd (Brookings, 1996), pp. 265–98.

9. William L. Sanders and June C. Rivers, *Cumulative and Residual Effects of Teachers on Future Student Academic Achievement* (Knoxville: University of Tennessee Value-Added Research and Assessment Center, 1996).

10. Linda Darling-Hammond, *Doing What Matters Most: Investing in Quality Teaching* (New York: National Commission on Teaching and America's Future, 1997).

11. For a review, see National Commission on Teaching and America's Future, *What Matters Most: Teaching for America's Future* (New York: Teachers College, Columbia University, 1996).

12. College Entrance Examination Board, *Equality and Excellence: The Educational Status of Black Americans* (New York, 1985); Lyle V. Jones, "White-Black Achievement Differences: The Narrowing Gap," *American Psychologist* 39 (1984), pp. 1207–13; Lyle V. Jones, N. W. Burton, and E. C. Davenport, "Monitoring the Achievement of Black Students," *Journal for Research in Mathematics Education* 15 (1984), pp. 154–64; E. G. Moore and A. W. Smith, "Mathematics Aptitude: Effects of Coursework, Household Language, and Ethnic Differences," *Urban Education* 20 (1985), pp. 273–94.

13. Robert Dreeben, "Closing the Divide: What Teachers and Administrators Can Do to Help Black Students Reach Their Reading Potential," *American Educator* 11 (4), pp. 28–35.

14. Eleanor Armour-Thomas and others, *An Outlier Study of Elementary and Middle Schools in New York City: Final Report* (New York City Board of Education, 1989).

15. Reviewed in Darling-Hammond, *The Right to Learn*.

16. National Commission on Teaching, *What Matters Most*.

17. Darling-Hammond, *Doing What Matters Most*.

18. Ibid.

19. Darling-Hammond, *The Right to Learn*.

eight   **Vouchers and Central City Schools**

Paul E. Peterson
Jay P. Greene

Some say that U.S. race relations are improving; others say they are not. Some say that affirmative action has fostered racial progress; others say it has not. But almost all Americans, liberal or conservative, agree that in the long run racial equality can be fully achieved only by eliminating disparities in the average educational performances of blacks and whites. Most Americans, we submit, would go so far as to say that if the next generation of blacks and whites acquire similar academic skills, the remaining barriers to racial equality could well slip away of their own accord. Despite this broad consensus for education's central importance, the United States tolerates the isolation of half of its African American children in unsafe and severely underperforming public schools. Any serious attempt to eliminate racial inequities must correct this glaring blot on the nation's racial report card.

Central City Schools

Half of all African Americans, but only 20 percent of whites, in public school attend central city schools. In the largest U.S. cities, the racial differences between central city and suburban schools are even more dramatic. In Chicago, Dallas, Detroit, Houston, Los Angeles, and Washington, more than 85 percent of public school students are of minority background.

Unfortunately, it is in these big cities that public schools fail their students most miserably and that the costs of failure are most severe. According to a national survey carried out in 1996, only 43 percent of urban students read at a basic level, compared with 63 percent of students in nonurban areas. Among high-poverty schools, the differences are even greater. Only 23 percent of students at urban high-poverty schools read at the basic level as compared with 46 percent in nonurban high-poverty areas.[1] Similar performances for urban schools are reported in math and science. As columnist William Raspberry put it in the *Washington Post*, "Poor children desperately need better education. Yet the schools they attend—particularly in America's overwhelmingly black and brown inner cities—may be the least successful of all public schools."[2]

In most big cities, average test scores fall as students advance through the public schools. For example, a *New York Times* article matched New York City students against statewide averages, controlling for students' racial and income status. It found that they scored three percentile points behind the statewide average in third grade, six percentile points behind in sixth grade, and as much as fifteen points behind in high school.[3] According to Department of Education statistics, the share of all students who go to private schools is much higher in big cities (15.8 percent) than in either suburban (11.7 percent) or rural (5.4 percent) areas.[4] Lacking the resources to follow suit, low-income central city families often find themselves forced to accept the school to which their child is assigned, leaving many dissatisfied. A 1997 *New York Times* article, for example, revealed that 93 percent of blacks in Denver agreed that "some children in the Denver public school system are receiving a substandard education."[5]

As evidence of urban school failure piles up, Urban League President Hugh Price has put big-city schools on notice: "If urban schools . . . continue to fail in the face of all we know about how to improve them, then [parents] will be obliged to shop elsewhere for quality education. We Urban Leaguers believe passionately in public education. But make no mistake. We love our children even more."[6]

Choice Schools

Fed up with central city schools, many African Americans are beginning to throw their support behind school vouchers. When Stanford professor Terry Moe conducted a nationwide survey of 4,700 parents, he found that school choice commands the greatest support in central cities: 90 percent of the inner-city poor favor a "voucher plan," compared with 60 percent of whites living in more advantaged communities; 61 percent of the inner-city poor "strongly" favor vouchers, as against just a third of the advantaged whites.[7]

A national survey of black and white Americans conducted in 1997 by the Joint Center of Political and Economic Studies also found the greatest support for vouchers among African Americans: 57 percent, as compared with 47 percent of white respondents.[8] Younger and poorer African Americans were the most supportive. Finally, a poll conducted by Phi Delta Kappa, a professional education association, found that 72 percent of black respondents favored vouchers, compared with just 48 percent of the general population.[9]

Given this support for vouchers, it is worth considering whether giving inner-city children a chance to go to a private school will make much difference. Studies of six state or privately funded voucher or scholarship programs that offer low-income, inner-city students a choice of private schools, religious or secular, provide some answers to often-asked questions.[10] The largest program is in Milwaukee; the others are in Cleveland, Dayton, Indianapolis, New York City, and Washington, D.C. (table 8-1).

Most students in these programs come from disadvantaged families. In all cities except Indianapolis most are likely to be African American. Most come from one-parent families. Many receive welfare, medicaid, food stamps, or other government assistance. Average test scores are well below national norms. However, a majority of students come from families in which at least one parent says he or she has had some college education.

Satisfaction with Choice Schools

Participating families love their choice schools. A year into the Cleveland choice program, parent Pamela Ballard exclaimed, "HOPE Acad-

Table 8-1. Characteristics of Major Big-City School Choice Programs for Low-Income Families

City	Sponsor	Religious schools included?	Grades	First school year	Initial enrollment	1998–99 enrollment	Number of schools	Maximum payment (dollars)	Selection method
Cleveland	State of Ohio	Yes	K–6	1996–97	1,996	3,600	55	2,500	Lottery
Dayton	PACE[a]	Yes	K–12	1998–99	542	542	35	1,200	Lottery
Indianapolis	ECCT[b]	Yes	K–8	1991–92	746	1,014[c]	70	800	First come
Milwaukee	State of Wisconsin	Yes	pre-K–12	1990–91	337	5,830	88	4,894	School-based lottery
New York City	SCSF[d]	Yes	1–5	1997–98	1,200	2,100	256	1,400	Lottery
Washington, D.C.	WSF[e]	Yes	pre-K–8	1993–94	57	1,200	110	2,200	Lottery

Source: See table 8-2.

a. Parents Advancing Choice in Education.
b. Educational Choice Charitable Trust.
c. 1996–97.
d. School Choice Scholarships Foundation.
e. Washington Scholarship Fund.

Table 8-2. Gains in Parental Satisfaction When Children Move to Choice Schools

Percent

Program	Teacher	Instruction	Discipline	Amount learned	Safety	Parental involvement
Cleveland[a]	31[b]	34[c]	22	n.a.	33	35
Dayton	43	46[d]	47	48[e]	39	38
Indianapolis[f]	25	39	40	32	n.a.	n.a.
Milwaukee[g]	1	16	16	16	n.a.	17
New York[h]	40	36[c]	43	40[i]	36	21
Washington, D.C.[j]	40	42[d]	44	40[e]	41	29

a. Jay P. Greene, Paul E. Peterson, and William Howell, "Preliminary Report on Cleveland School Scholarship Program," Harvard University, Kennedy School of Government, Program on Education Policy and Governance, 1997. Difference between parents of applicants winning scholarship and of applicants not selected who remained in public schools. Percentage "very satisfied."

b. Question asked about satisfaction with "private attention to child."

c. Question asked about satisfaction with "academic quality."

d. Question asked about "academic quality."

e. Percentage giving school a grade of "A" for how well student is taught.

f. David J. Weinschrott and Sally B. Kilgore, "Evidence from the Indianapolis Voucher Program," in *Learning from School Choice*, edited by Paul E. Peterson and Bryan C. Hassel (Brookings, 1998), pp. 307–34. Gain after two years among parents who were satisfied and very satisfied with the choice school.

g. John F. Witte and others, "Fourth-Year Report: Milwaukee Parental Choice Program," Robert LaFollette Institute of Public Affairs, University of Wisconsin—Madison, December 1994, table A6. Average gain for the first four years among parents who were very satisfied with the choice school.

h. Paul E. Peterson, David Myers, and William G. Howell, "An Evaluation of the New York City School Choice Scholarships Program: The First Year," Program on Education Policy and Governance Report 98-12, Kennedy School of Government, 1998, table 15.

i. "What is taught in school."

j. Paul E. Peterson, Jay P. Greene, William G. Howell, and William McCready, "Initial Findings from an Evaluation of School Choice Programs in Washington, D.C. and Dayton, Ohio." Paper presented before annual meetings of the Association of Public Policy and Management, New York City, October 1998.

n.a. Not available.

emy was my last hope. I took my third-grade child, who had been in several Cleveland schools and was labeled a problem child. I now have a successful child. Where there were Ds and Cs, there are now As and Bs." Ballard's enthusiasm represents the norm, not the exception. According to studies in six cities, choice schools are more popular than public schools (see table 8-2).

The studies use slightly different methodologies and ask somewhat different questions—some about teachers and instruction, others about the amount learned, discipline, safety, and parental involvement—but the results do not depend much on the methodology or the question. Almost always, parents prefer choice schools to public schools, usually by large margins.

Impartial observers agree with parents' positive assessments. In Milwaukee, for example, a reporter for *Education Week* reached much the same conclusions that Milwaukee parents did: "Classes here are highly structured and yet free of regimentation; there is a sense of order, yet order itself is not the point. The activities are purposeful; the students, enthusiastic participants."[11] A seventh grader in a Carnegie Foundation for the Advancement of Teaching interview made the most convincing case for her new school: "As soon as I came here it was a big change. Here, teachers care about you. . . . [In public school] the teachers were too busy to help." Worst of all, she said, were the fights: "You really can't avoid it. They'll think you're scared."[12]

Most revealing of all, school teachers are more likely than the average central city resident to pick a private school for their own son or daughter. As Dennis Doyle noted in a 1995 report for the Center for Education Reform, 40 percent of the children of Cleveland public school teachers go to private school, as compared with 25 percent of all children.[13] In Milwaukee the percentages are 33, as compared with 23, in Boston 45, as compared with 29.

Test Scores in Choice Schools

Students also seem to learn more in choice schools. In Cleveland, for example, students in two schools (that enrolled about 25 percent of the former public school students) made significant gains in both math and reading.[14] The Cleveland findings, however, may be contaminated by what is known as the selection effect. After all, families who are clever and motivated enough to get a scholarship are likely to have other attributes that spur their children's educational attainment. However, data available from the choice experiment in Milwaukee, where the students applying for choice were assigned to a test or control group by means of a lottery, show that a student's enrollment in the program had only modest effects during the first two years. By years three and four, however, choice students began outstripping their peers in the control group. If such gains can be duplicated nationwide, they could reduce by between one-third and one-half of the current difference between white and minority test score performance.[15]

It should not be surprising that student performance does not improve considerably until the third and fourth years. Choice schools are not magic bullets. Education does not happen overnight; it takes time to adjust to a new teaching and learning environment. The disruption of switching schools and adjusting to new routines and expectations may hamper improvement in test scores in the first year or two in a choice school. Educational benefits accumulate and multiply with the passage of time.

Significant gains were observed after just one year for fourth and fifth graders in the New York City choice program. Once again, these gains are of special note because the choice students were compared to public school students similar to the choice students except that they had not won a scholarship in a lottery. Although stable differences between the two groups of students were not observed in the early grades, the private school advantage was noticeable for fourth and fifth graders: three percentile points in reading and six in mathematics. If these effects increase at this rate in subsequent years (a matter we are now investigating), then the educational impact on minority students will be very large. Even after one year, it appears as if the lower levels of conflict and disruption that parents observe in private schools has a particularly large educational effect on inner-city students as they enter the middle-school years.[16]

Democratic Values and Balkanization

Choice critics point out that the purpose of education is not merely to teach math and reading but also to prepare citizens for a democratic society. According to critics such as former *New Republic* editor Michael Kelly, "Public money is shared money, and it is to be used for the furtherance of shared values, in the interests of e pluribus unum. Charter schools and their like . . . take from the pluribus to destroy the unum."[17] It was, after all, not so long ago that choice privatization was a strategy favored by those seeking to avoid compliance with the Supreme Court's 1954 *Brown* v. *Board of Education* decision. Other courts went on to strike down these misguided attempts to perpetuate racial segregation, precluding such strategies in the future.

The evidence from most private schools today is that privatization leads to less balkanization, not more. Today's private school students are less racially isolated than their public school peers. According to 1992 Department of Education data, 37 percent of private school students are in classrooms whose share of minority students is close to the national average, compared with only 18 percent of public school students.[18] Not only are private school students more likely to be in well-integrated classrooms, they are less likely to be in extremely segregated ones (either more than 90 percent white or more than 90 percent minority). Forty-one percent of private school students are in highly segregated classrooms, as compared with 55 percent of their public school peers.

Private school students also report more positive relationships with students from other racial and ethnic groups. According to the same 1992 survey, they are significantly more likely to have cross-racial friendships than are students at public schools. Students, teachers, and administrators at private schools all report fewer racial problems. Private school students are also more community spirited. According to the 1992 survey, students at private schools are more likely than public school students to think that it is important to help others and volunteer for community causes. They also are more likely to report that they in fact did volunteer in the past two years and to say their school expected them to do so.

The Church-State Question

On the church-state question, federal constitutional questions may not pose as much of a stumbling block to school choice as they once did, despite some lower-court decisions to the contrary. State-provided scholarships do not "establish a religion" as long as parents are free to use them to send their children to any school, Catholic, Protestant, Jewish, Muslim, or secular. The Supreme Court so reasoned in 1983 (*Mueller v. Allen*) when it ruled constitutional a Minnesota tax deduction for educational expenses, whether for secular or parochial schooling. It reaffirmed that reasoning in *Agostini v. Felton* (1997) when it said that public school teachers could provide compensatory educational instruction in parochial schools. The Court conditioned its decision on policies that made instruction "available generally without regard to the sectarian-nonsectarian or public-nonpublic nature of the institution benefitted," further justifying its decision on the grounds that no religion was aided except as the result of the "private choices of individuals." State supreme courts in Wisconsin and Ohio have ruled that school choice programs pass such a test, and the Supreme Court chose not to review the Wisconsin decision, thereby keeping the voucher program intact.

The Effect on Public Schools

But how about those left behind? American Federation of Teachers President Sandra Feldman has said that vouchers and scholarships for private schools take "money away from inner-city schools so a few selected children can get vouchers to attend private schools, while the majority of equally deserving kids, who remain in the public schools, are ignored."[19] Yet there is little reason to expect the best and the brightest to flee the public schools to take advantage of inner-city choice programs. For one thing, most big-city school systems have their own special programs—magnet schools, gifted classes, and honors tracks—that siphon off the best students. Also, parents can be expected not to change their children's school unless they have doubts about their progress. In New York City, only 26 percent of those applying for choice schools scored at grade level on the reading test, far below the 55 percent of all elementary school students scoring at that level as reported by the city's school system.

The creaming of inner-city public schools took place long before school choice arrived on the public agenda. In America's biggest cities, the middle-class population has already left for suburbia or for private schools. Indeed, one attraction of inner-city school choice is the possibility that it could reduce racial isolation within the central city.

Speaking to a Pittsburgh conference on urban renewal, Milwaukee's visionary mayor, John Norquist, argued that if school choice becomes a reality, "public schools will respond to private sector competition with an aggressive effort to maintain their clientele, just as United and American Airlines did."[20] Empowered to choose among a variety of schools, young parents with children entering school will forgo the expensive move to the suburbs and pick instead a local school suited to their needs. Other families, offered better schools in the cities, will give up their suburban homes to live closer to their jobs. Businesses will open schools so their employees can bring their children with them on their daily commute. The central city economy will pick up, property values will rise, racial integration will increase, and central city test scores will rise.

Schools and Government Responsibility

School choice is not a panacea that can resolve all of society's race-related problems. It will not by itself eliminate all the differences in the educational performances of racial groups. Much of what we know, we learn not in school but from our families, friends, and myriad other life experiences. Schools are, however, one of the most important sources available to the government for the amelioration of racial inequity.

Unfortunately, many have come to believe that for government to achieve that objective, it must directly operate the educational system it finances, even though government often can better achieve its goals by mobilizing the energies of churches, nonprofit organizations, and profit-making institutions. In most policy arenas—transportation, health services, scientific research, pollution control—that is the strategy government typically follows. Now, when government-operated institutions such as central city schools have fallen into a serious state of disrepair, it is even more crucial that government find alternative ways of achieving common objectives. As William Raspberry urgently recommends: "It's time for some serious experimentation."[21]

Notes

1. Lynn Olson and Craig D. Jerald, "'The Achievement Gap,' The Urban Challenge: Public Education in the Fifty States," *Education Week: Editorial Projects in Education*, January 8, 1998, pp. 10–13.

2. William Raspberry, "A Reluctant Convert to School Choice," *Washington Post*, May 20, 1997; reprinted in Thomas B. Fordham Foundation, *Selected Readings on School Reform* 1 (Summer 1997), p. 13.

3. Pam Belluck, "Learning Gap Tied to Time in the System: As School Stay Grows, Scores on Tests Worsen," *New York Times*, January 5, 1997.

4. Robin R. Henke and others, *Schools and Staffing in the United States: A Statistical Profile* (Government Printing Office, 1996), p. 17.

5. James Brooke, "Minorities Flock to Cause of Vouchers for Schools," *New York Times*, December 27, 1997.

6. Paul E. Peterson, "Top Ten Questions Asked about School Choice," in *Brookings Papers on Education Policy*, edited by Diane Ravitch (Brookings, 1999), p. 405.

7. The question was worded, "According to reformers, the general idea behind a voucher plan is as follows: The parents of each school-age child would be eligible for a grant or voucher from the state, representing a certain amount of tax money. They would have the right to send their child to a public school, just as before. Or they could use the voucher to help pay for the child's education at a private or parochial school of their choosing." Terry Moe, *Schools, Vouchers, and Public Opinion* (Brookings, forthcoming).

8. Joint Center for Political and Economic Studies, *1997 National Opinion Poll* (Washington, D.C., 1977), table 7.

9. Brooke, "Minorities Flock to Cause of Vouchers."

10. John F. Witte and others, "Fourth-Year Report: Milwaukee Parental Choice Program" (University of Wisconsin—Madison, Robert LaFollette Institute of Public Affairs, 1994); David J. Weinschrott and Sally B. Kilgore, "Evidence from the Indianapolis Voucher Program," in *Learning from School Choice*, edited by Paul E. Peterson and Bruce C. Hassel (Brookings, 1998), pp. 307–34; Jay P. Greene, Paul E. Peterson, and William Howell, "Preliminary Report on Cleveland School Scholarship Program" (Kennedy School of Government, Program on Education Policy and Governance, 1997); Paul E. Peterson, David Myers, and William G. Howell, "An Evaluation of the New York City School Choice Scholarships Program: The First Year" (Kennedy School of Government, Program on Education Policy and Governance, 1998); Paul E. Peterson and others, "Initial Findings from an Evaluation of School Choice Programs in Washington, D.C., and Dayton, Ohio," paper prepared for annual meetings of the Association of Public Policy and Management, New York City, October 1998.

11. David Ruenzel, "A Choice in the Matter," *Education Week*, September 27, 1995, p. 28.

12. Carnegie Foundation for the Advancement of Teaching, *School Choice: A Special Report* (Princeton, N.J., 1992), p. 69.

13. Dennis P. Doyle, "Where Connoisseurs Send Their Children to School" (Washington, D.C.: Center for Education Reform, 1995), reprinted in *A Choice for Our Children: Curing the Crisis in America's Schools,* edited by Alan Bonsteel and

Carlos A. Bonilla (San Francisco: Institute for Contemporary Studies, 1997), pp. 40–41.

14. Jay P. Greene, William G. Howell, and Paul E. Peterson, "Lessons from the Cleveland Scholarship Program," in *Learning from School Choice*, edited by Paul E. Peterson and Bryan C. Hassel (Brookings, 1998), pp. 357–94. Also see Paul E. Peterson, William G. Howell, and Jay P. Greene, "An Evaluation of the Cleveland Voucher Program after Two Years" (John Kennedy School of Government, Program on Education Policy and Governance, June 1999).

15. Jay P. Greene, Paul E. Peterson, and Jiangtao Du, "School Choice in Milwaukee: A Randomized Experiment," in *Learning from School Choice*, edited by Paul E. Peterson and Bryan C. Hassel (Brookings, 1998), pp. 335–56.

16. Paul E. Peterson and others, "Effects of School Choice in New York City," in *Earning and Learning: How Schools Matter*, edited by Susan B. Mayer and Paul E. Peterson (Brookings, 1999), pp. 319–42.

17. Michael Kelly, "Dangerous Minds," *New Republic*, December 30, 1996.

18. These findings and others are reported in Jay P. Greene, "Civic Values in Public and Private Schools," in *Learning from School Choice*, edited by Paul E. Peterson and Bryan C. Hassel (Brookings, 1998), pp. 83–106.

19. Sandra Feldman, "Let's Tell the Truth," *New York Times*, November 2, 1997. Advertisement.

20. John Norquist, presentation before the Conference on Urban Renewal, Carnegie-Mellon University, July 2, 1997.

21. Raspberry, "A Reluctant Convert to School Choice."

part four

Community

nine   **Impediments to**
Integration

Nathan Glazer

A sharp residential separation of whites and blacks, documented statistically in research, could be observed in most American cities in the
1950s and 1960s. That separation, which could also be described as
"segregation,"[1] was already under attack in the 1960s and 1970s by
a variety of new federal policies emerging from all three branches of
government. In his 1973 book *Opening up the Suburbs*, Anthony
Downs had even more extensive policies to propose.[2] Some twenty-
five years ago, I argued that all this was unnecessary: blacks would
become residentially more integrated with whites as their economic
circumstances improved, as their political power increased, and as
they drew closer in all other respects to whites.[3] We could expect this
to happen as a result of the powerful antidiscrimination legislation
of 1964, 1965, and 1968.

Whatever the changes that have occurred in the black condition
since that time, in this one respect—the degree of concentration of
blacks in specific areas of cities and some selected suburbs and the
residential isolation of blacks in general—there has been little change.

This chapter is adapted from Nathan Glazer, *We Are All Multiculturists Now*
(Harvard University Press), by permission of the author and reprinted by permission of the publisher, copyright © 1997 by the President and Fellows of Harvard College.

In many respects, the commonly held expectations of the 1960s and 1970s as to the future of blacks and of black-white relations have not been fulfilled. Had one been asked at the time of the passage of the Civil Rights Act in 1964 to project how matters would stand thirty years in the future, what well-informed person would have predicted the degree of separation between blacks and whites that now exists in residence, in economic conditions, in family patterns, and in attitudes?

There were good reasons to believe in the mid-1970s that the pattern of residential concentration and isolation would erode. Thus further governmental interventions—whether to strengthen the prohibition of discrimination in rental, sales, and realtor behavior; to impose integration on new developments; or to integrate housing projects through public measures—were not necessary. We could have argued over whether the measures then in force proscribing discrimination in sales and rentals and segregation in government-assisted housing should be stronger, but it seemed to me in 1974 that the processes of social change, abetted by the expected continuing and increased economic and social mobility of blacks, would change the pattern of black segregation.

One has to go back twenty-five years and get a sense of the period to make the case that at the time these views seemed justifiable, that there was good reason to believe that the remarkable 1960s revolution in civil rights law would spur the improvement in the economic, educational, housing, and neighborhood conditions of American blacks that had to a substantial degree already been evident in the postwar period.

Ben Wattenberg and others at the time published articles demonstrating the increased percentage of blacks becoming middle-class in occupation and earnings.[4] Irving Kristol wrote an article in 1966, "The Negro Today Is Like the Immigrant Yesterday," a title that would strike us now with a certain irony but that made perfect sense at the time.[5] It made sense to me. I implied the same in *Beyond the Melting Pot*, in 1963.[6] Of course when we spoke of immigrants in the mid-1960s we were not thinking about *new* immigrants to the United States—we were comparing Negroes to the immigrants of the past. Despite the passage of an immigration reform act in 1965, the immigrants were then people of yesterday, and no one expected that mass immigration to the United States would resume in the future.

One had reason in 1966, or ten years later, to expect that American Negroes, as they were then called, would follow the course of early European immigrants, the "tenement trail," as Samuel Lubell called it.[7] After all, American Negroes were still relative newcomers, compared with European immigrants, in the cities of the North and West, and now that we had powerful civil rights legislation, what would prevent their rise?

There were advocates for further federal measures, greater than those already in place, in education, housing, employment training, income support, and other areas to improve conditions in cities and for American blacks, but we were already in a period of federal (and state and local) fiscal constraint, from which we have only recently emerged. There had in any case already been a great expansion of federal programs in the 1960s and 1970s. Thus in the field of housing segregation alone the Fair Housing Act of 1968 was supplemented in 1974 by the Housing and Community Development Act, which required communities to prepare a detailed "housing assistance plan," taking account of the needs of low-income families, before receiving federal grants. The Equal Credit Opportunity Act of 1974 prohibited discrimination in home lending and required banks to compile information on the race of loan applicants and recipients. A 1976 court order required three federal agencies to collect racial data on home loan applicants, and the 1975 Home Mortgage Disclosure Act required banks to report on the neighborhood pattern of their loans. The 1977 Community Reinvestment Act required banks to demonstrate that they were providing loans to low-income areas. One could undoubtedly recite other measures.

Was more necessary to assist the rise of blacks? Twenty-five years ago, one could believe, as I did, that more was not necessary—that the measures banning discrimination in employment, education, housing, and government programs were sufficient; that the agencies policing these measures were competent; that the civil rights groups watching the agencies were vigilant; that the courts that would respond to their complaints on effectiveness of enforcement were sympathetic. One could believe that American blacks would follow the path of European immigrants, now that state-imposed restrictions were lifted and private discrimination in key areas was banned.

Others did believe that more was necessary, and Anthony Downs was among them. The federal government was then engaged, as it still is, in efforts to go beyond the banning of overt and direct discrimination. We had extensive efforts at integration—in employment, through affirmative action; in education, through cases calling for desegregation through busing; in housing, where various schemes and programs were afoot to better integrate publicly subsidized housing and to require integration in private development. To such intrusive measures of integration I was opposed, and I expressed this opposition in my 1975 book *Affirmative Discrimination*. European immigrants had not needed them, I argued, and American blacks would not need them as their educational attainment increased, their earnings rose, and they entered white-collar and professional and managerial occupations in greater numbers. Integration in schools and colleges and in housing and residence would follow in due course.

There was a good deal of ignorance of the ethnic and racial patterns of American life, I asserted, in those who saw every degree of separation of blacks from whites as the result of prejudice and discrimination and set as the proper measure of equality the even distribution of blacks in all areas of life. There was an equal measure of ignorance of our ethnic and racial history among those who assumed that the breakup of concentrations by government action was necessary for black advancement. No ethnic or racial group had shown such an even distribution. Black concentrations could have been matched by Jewish or Italian concentrations earlier in the century. In every group there was some tendency to prefer propinquity to family and friends and churches and social institutions. Differences in tastes, culture, and income led to different patterns of institutional facilities and local businesses in residential neighborhoods. Many factors quite independent of prejudice and discrimination made some clustering of ethnic and racial groups inevitable and indeed natural. A decent respect for freedom of association and for the differences among people should be observed by government, and it should stand back from efforts to push the desired objective of integration. Integration would happen in any case, as a result of economic, political, and social changes that were inevitable.

These views, whatever evidence could have been collected to support them in the middle 1970s, now strike me as complacent. A unique degree of separation continues to divide blacks from other Americans. The facts have been developed most starkly and presented most effectively by Douglas Massey and Nancy Denton in *American Apartheid*.[8] Thirty years after the civil rights revolution and the revolutionary change in the legal posture affecting discrimination, the situation can only be described as extremely depressing. The authors develop measures of both segregation and isolation, calculated on different bases and reflecting somewhat different realities, but the picture for both indexes reflects so high a degree of separation that it is hardly necessary to go into the details.

Comparing 1970 and 1980, they write: "Among the oldest and largest northern ghettoes . . . there was virtually no sign of progress in residential integration. In Boston, Chicago, Cleveland, Detroit, Gary, Philadelphia, Pittsburgh and St. Louis, the decline in the segregation index was 4 points or less, and in two metropolitan areas (New York and Newark) segregation actually *increased* over the decade." There were more substantial declines in Columbus, Los Angeles, and San Francisco, but the authors attribute these declines to "unusual instability in housing patterns caused by a combination of gentrification, immigration, and rapid housing construction rather than to an ongoing process of neighborhood racial integration."[9]

All the more benign explanations of this remarkable stability of racial segregation collapse on investigation. Is this the pattern we might expect from new immigrants or new migrants into cities? Recency of migration does not explain it: black communities in the North and West are no longer fed by heavy immigration from the South, and this has been the case for twenty years or more. Nevertheless, the authors tell us, the levels of segregation in northern cities in 1980 were above the highest ever recorded for European ethnic groups.

Is this the same pattern we find for other nonwhite groups—is it a general "minority" pattern? As in the case of intermarriage, it is not: "The high level of segregation experienced by blacks today is . . . unique compared with the experience of other large minority groups, such as Hispanics and Asians."[10] Black residential isolation is as out of line compared with Asian or Hispanic patterns as black intermarriage is.

Is this only a central city pattern, and can we expect its mitigation as more blacks move into suburbs? Perhaps we can, but black suburbanization increases very slowly. The overwhelming majority of blacks are still in central cities. Insofar as suburbanization has increased, much of it has been into suburban areas that are in effect extensions of central city black areas or into suburbs that have become dominantly black. Black segregation is lower when we consider the suburban areas of metropolitan areas as a whole—but not markedly lower.

Is this pattern mitigated for blacks of higher income? Not at all. Segregation is as severe for those with incomes above $50,000 as for those below.

Is it the effect of black desires, black tastes? Do blacks prefer to live in black areas? Not really. Blacks have been asked in public opinion surveys what kind of neighborhood they would prefer to live in: "By large majorities, blacks support the ideal of integration and express a preference for integrated living, and 95% are willing to live in neighborhoods that are anywhere between 15% and 70% black."

Here we do have a problem in the interaction between black desires as to the level of integration blacks would find comfortable or prefer and the level whites would find comfortable or prefer. Massey and Denton report that many surveys show that "blacks strongly prefer a 50-50 mixture, and that whites have little tolerance for racial mixture beyond 20% black." The relationship between these preferences results in instability. I am not suggesting that the proportion of black and white in a neighborhood is the only factor or even necessarily the decisive factor in decisions to move out of or into a neighborhood. In a society of high mobility such as ours, however—with almost one-fifth of the households of the country moving every year—even a modest preference in the residential racial mix desired will, over time, lead to a concentration of blacks in one or a few areas.

Thomas Schelling elegantly demonstrated this twenty-five years ago.[11] Take a checkerboard, he said, and distribute nickels and dimes on it at random, with 10 percent of the coins nickels, leaving a few spaces empty. Then move one coin at a time into an empty space, with only this rule: the nickel would like to have at least one of its neighboring spaces occupied by a nickel, the dime would like to have one of its neighboring spaces occupied by a dime. In a relatively few moves, the nickels begin to concentrate in one section of the checkerboard. If the preference is for two neighboring nickels or for two neighboring dimes, the concentration will occur faster.

What underlies this process? To Massey and Denton, it is prejudice. To me, the matter is more complicated. It is preference and is based on a range of factors. In some cases, particularly in white working-class neighborhoods, we will indeed find prejudice, intense and direct. This is well documented in studies of such neighborhoods; but one scarcely needs the studies—newspaper reports are evidence enough.[12] This prejudice is based to some degree on the experience of such communities with low-income blacks in their neighborhoods. It is not easy to separate out from prejudice the influence of fears that, with an increase in black occupancy, crime will increase, schools will decline, and house values will drop. In enlightened middle-class neighborhoods, with a commitment to the ideal of integration, the fears of what kind of change will occur with an increase in black occupancy may have little to do with prejudice, as ordinarily understood. In these neighborhoods, however, there will also be fears that crime will increase, property values will decline, and schools will become poorer.[13] These fears are shared by both blacks and whites. There is little difference between blacks and whites in their expectation that more blacks will mean more crime and a decline in property values.

Whether low-income or middle-income, prejudiced or unprejudiced, neighborhoods will organize, using different methods and appeals, to restrain an increase in black occupancy. When houses are the largest part of the wealth of a family, it is understandable that homeowners will act with as much caution as bondholders, who are ready to move billions of dollars on the basis of fears that to many of us appear minuscule.

The Schelling demonstration that small preferences (or, if you will, a relatively modest degree of prejudice) may produce large effects may save American society from the charge of being irredeemably racist, but the consequences, in terms of separation and segregation, appear to be remarkably similar. Working-class attitudes may be more prejudiced than middle-class attitudes (in any case, the expression of prejudice is more direct and unmodulated), but middle-class behavior will still aim at either the exclusion of blacks or the restriction of black entry into an area. If exclusion or restriction fails, the area will often rapidly become almost totally black. The sharp decline in the racist sentiments of the American population in the past thirty years—and I do not dismiss this decline as simply a matter of being polite and proper to the opinion poll-sters—has done remarkably little to change the overall pattern of black concentration, of black isolation from the rest of the population. Schelling's demonstration explains in part why such a sharp decline in negative attitudes can have such modest effects on the overall pattern of segregation, but the segregation remains.

Segregation has, I believe, serious consequences, even though social scientists continue to debate whether there is a contagion effect, whether the indexes of dysfunction among the black poor would be the same or different if they were spread out and integrated rather than concentrated and isolated.[14] Just how to sort out the influences of poverty, lack of jobs, lack of role models, high concentration, poor schools, and other factors that make the black inner-city ghetto what it is today is not simple. Yet it stands to reason that if the black poor could be redistributed so that their neighbors, black or white, were often not poor, it would help. There is some research evidence that common sense on this matter is not mis-taken, but whatever the more sophisticated research concludes, most of us believe the segregation of the black poor in the central cities has seri-ous consequences. Those behaviors with which we are all familiar from television and the newspapers—a high rate of crime, juvenile delinquency, poor school performance, out-of-wedlock births, and the rest—must be accentuated by the effect of concentration alone, even though social sci-entists are not yet agreed that they can demonstrate this independent effect.

Yet another effect of the separation of the races is seen in language and, at the extreme, the capacity to communicate. Of course any group develops a distinctive vocabulary, idioms, formulations, intonations, but the black poor seem to be drifting further away from standard English, very likely an effect of isolation and concentration, and this adds an addi-tional burden to the efforts to break out of the ghetto and poverty.

For the most part blacks and whites understand one another well enough, across the barriers of race and class. A different style of Eng-lish, however, particularly if it is associated with a historically lower caste, communicates something as to class, attitude, community, and a host of other factors, which add up to a sense of difference—the kind of difference that suggests the possibility of trouble to the dominant caste. Despite the overwhelming presence of the mass media, which should lead to more uniformity, speech variants drift further apart. Speech patterns are apparently better communicated orally by one's close associates from childhood, with whom one is in direct face-to-face contact, than by the TV set or the school. As a leading sociolinguist, William Labov, writes on the basis of studies in Philadelphia and elsewhere:

> The black population does not participate in the rapid evolution of the white vernacular. . . . As the sound pattern of the Philadelphia white community becomes more and more different from the speech of Boston, Chicago, and Fort Worth, it is also becoming more and more different from the sound pattern used by black Philadelphians. We find the same situation in all the large Northern cities. . . . The local white accents show rapid divergence from each other, while the black communities remain aloof. Instead of increased differentiation, the black sound pattern shows a generalized Northern black phonology.[15]

This research on language is intriguing, but a resort to common experience on this point is as persuasive. Thirty years after the great effort in public law to bring us together, does one detect any lessening of the distinctive patterns of black English among the black poor or among the young blacks often featured in television programs on one or another social or educational problem? If anything, they are maintained and strengthened. A related phenomenon is the well-documented pattern in black ghetto schools of hostility to academic achievement; achieving academic success is considered "acting white." Speaking the common English of the TV anchor would also be considered acting white. These behaviors are undoubtedly spurred by ideological changes—by the shift in the attitudes of black leadership, and blacks generally—away from the assumption that blacks should act more like whites in order to progress toward the goal of assimilation. Instead we find support for various degrees of distinctiveness and difference—the rise of a distinc-

tive black identity in which the abandonment of linguistic distinctiveness may be seen as a form of group betrayal. This is interpreted differently at different class levels, and the signs of continuing group solidarity
vary enormously as one moves from ghetto youths to corporate lawyers.
Even in the most elite groups, however, some sign of linguistic distinctiveness, however attenuated, is commonly maintained.

Separation as well as differences in interest contribute to blacks and
whites coming to see the world differently. The surprisingly large diver-
gence that was shown in public opinion polls between blacks and non-
blacks as to O. J. Simpson's guilt is only the most striking of these
differences in how blacks and whites see the world. (It was driven home
to whites in the course of this trial just why blacks had good reason to
view the police and the system of justice differently from whites.) Recently
it has been noted that black and white television viewers are growing
further apart in the programs they favor. Separation in residence and
schooling is only one factor leading to these different interests and ori-
entations. Television producers seek to appeal to niche audiences, particularly if they form very large niches, as is the case with blacks, who
watch television more than whites. As the reporter of this phenomenon
writes, "the change is driven as much by the competitive pressures that
networks are feeling as any social or cultural factors," according to TV
executives and others.[16] Blacks and whites may have different views even
when they live next door to each other, but I believe residential and school
isolation makes a considerable contribution to these stark differences in
outlook.

It is at this point—when we lay out the facts, which cannot be
explained away, and when we lay out the consequences, about which
we can still argue—that the difficult part begins. What is to be done?
Can anything be done? Should anything be done? If under a regime of
freedom in which racial discrimination is banned and often punished,
blacks remain separate from whites, might that not be an indication of
the fact that over these twenty-five years the desire to retain something
distinctive that characterizes blacks—differences that may have been created by a tragic history but that despite that have become valued signs
of identity—has grown? The black of today is not the immigrant of yesterday (or of today, who assimilates probably at the same rate as the

immigrants of yesterday). To many blacks, a high degree of separation in intermarriage, residence, and language may describe a faultline in American society that is a social reality rather than a problem. This is one possible way of interpreting and responding to these facts.

If indeed that separation was chosen by those who have the opportunity and ability to choose otherwise, then there might be nothing more to say. Conceivably we might view the separation of blacks from whites the way we view the separation from the larger society of the Amish or of Hasidic Jews—but such comparison would be specious. When we speak of blacks, we are speaking of a group that is one-eighth of American society, not a tiny minority, and a group that is deeply implicated in the central themes of our history. Its major figures have always fought for integration into American life, whatever the power of separatist thinking among some members of the black community. Black separatism is largely a reaction to what is seen as white rejection, a failure of the larger society to integrate blacks.

Separation is not for the most part voluntarily chosen. It is the product of the interaction of poverty, social dysfunction, and the reaction of others to these problems. Separateness among middle-class blacks, whether self-selected or the product of that subtle interaction of differences in taste that Schelling analyzes, would be a different, and lesser, problem than the involuntary separateness of the black poor.

We should also not exaggerate the degree of this separation. Massey and Denton's segregation index (which "gives the percentage of all blacks who would have to move to achieve an even residential configuration— where each census tract replicates the racial composition of the metropolitan area as a whole") for the thirty metropolitan areas with the largest black populations averages 80 percent for the North and West and 68 percent for the South in 1980.[17] This shows some degree of integration, and some change since 1970, from averages of 85 and 75 percent, respectively. The isolation indexes, which "state the percentage of blacks living in the tract of the average African-American" and "measure the extent to which blacks live only among other blacks and gauge the potential for interracial contact within neighborhoods," are considerably lower, even outside the South—66 percent in the North and West and 64 percent in the South.

Perhaps one could argue on the basis of these figures that one-third of blacks are residentially integrated. Other data suggest a degree of integration that is considerably greater. Surprisingly, "almost 80 percent of blacks claim 'a good friend' who is white and high-status blacks are especially likely to make such claims," according to a survey by the National Conference of Christians and Jews.[18] In contrast, the reality of our inner cities (and these need not be very large cities) informs us, independently of indexes, that the degree of separation of blacks is unique in our culture. A generation ago we thought that the increase in the education and income and occupational level of blacks would ameliorate the problem, as long as we policed against discrimination, and that we would end up with concentrations of blacks no greater than could be seen among other ethnic and racial groups. It did not happen.

Proposing activist policies to promote integration is generally the way in which such a discussion ends. That is the way Anthony Downs ends *Opening up the Suburbs*, and that is the way Massey and Denton end *American Apartheid*. Such proposals exude an air of futility even as they are offered; whatever the policy, we have had some experience with it and know the inherent difficulties. One can require public housing agencies to promote racial integration. One can require that new developments put aside a certain percentage of units for low-income families or for blacks. These requirements can be variously federal, state, local, or judicial. One can require banks to provide more mortgages for blacks to buy in nonblack areas. One can require secondary mortgage agencies to pressure those banks to provide more mortgages for blacks to buy in nonblack areas. One can require government oversight agencies to monitor secondary mortgage agencies' pressure on banks to issue more mortgages for blacks to buy in nonblack areas. And so on and so on. One can be very ingenious in finding ways in which government, involved in so many parts of our lives, can bring its power into effect to encourage integration. A whole vocabulary has grown up around such efforts.[19]

Even as one spells out the litany of possible activist interventions, the accompanying objections, and difficulties in implementing them, unrolls before the eye of anyone who has had any experience with these efforts. As in the case of school busing, partially implemented, doubtfully successful, and now increasingly abandoned, government measures inspired by an ideal of fairness, equality, and integration cannot overcome the stubborn commitments of parents to what they consider best for their own children and neighborhood. Against these bedrock sentiments, all of government's good intentions, all well-designed public policies, crumble.

The best of these may have negative consequences. Efforts to integrate public housing projects have frequently placed elderly whites (because other poor whites were not available) next door to young black families, which has provided a difficult environment for the elderly and only reinforced their prejudices against blacks. Sometimes when private developers of rental projects have made special efforts to recruit white tenants in order to maintain an integrated community, they have been sued by the NAACP or the government for discriminating against blacks. This is what happened to Starrett City in Brooklyn.[20] If liberal suburban neighborhoods, seeing a slow drift to black majority residence, make special efforts to recruit white families when houses becomes available, by advertising their community to whites and creating programs to assist white families to move in, how different from discrimination will that appear to civil rights agencies or indeed to black neighbors? Neither black civil rights organizations nor government agencies may be willing to make the distinction between discriminating against and trying to maintain integration with, and indeed the distinction is not easy to make: activist community efforts to maintain an integrated community require discrimination.

There are creative programs: guaranteeing to white homeowners that the value of their property will not fall, for example. How different, though, is that from discrimination? How extensive can such programs be? How effective can they be, when homeowners hope for unrealistic increases in the value of their property?

In Boston in the 1970s the mayor and the banks agreed to make a major commitment to provide below-rate mortgages to blacks moving into a white middle- and lower-income homeowning community. A Jewish neighborhood was selected for this large program, to reduce the chances of violence against entering blacks. The primary objective was improving housing conditions among blacks, but certainly there was no expectation that the neighborhood would become all black; integration was also the goal. Then real estate agents moved in, frightening the whites in the neighborhood, urging them to get out fast before blacks moved in, and pressuring black families to take mortgages they could not afford. One can spell out the rest. The neighborhood declined rapidly; the ghetto expanded.[21] Perhaps the program was implemented poorly, but one cannot deny the good intentions. Even the somewhat suspicious chroniclers and analysts of this debacle accept that there were good intentions.

Whatever the virtue of these and other policies—and their virtues are to be found generally more in the intentions of their implementers than in their effects—who can expect them to be adopted on any large scale in the present political mood or indeed in any foreseeable future political mood? The two Democratic administrations that have leavened decades of Republican presidential dominance have been understandably more sympathetic to such measures than the Republican administrations, but very little has been accomplished. The history of policy efforts to integrate neighborhoods and communities has been one of many schemes, of extended and endless litigation, and of very small successes.

Yet there have been successes—small scale, painful, often expensive— in the maintenance of integrated residential neighborhoods, generally upper middle class, and to move central city blacks out of concentrated areas. Richard Taub and his collaborators document some of the former in Chicago, a highly segregated city.[22] We have seen similar efforts with variable success in the St. Louis and Cleveland areas and elsewhere.[23] Taub also documents how perilous, how much on the edge, these successes are, if the measure is the maintenance of integration. They often require heavy institutional commitments, such as those by the University of Chicago, and such actors are available in only a few neighborhoods. The successes are assisted by the inherent attractiveness of housing in some neighborhoods, which generally means older housing, built at a time when size and ornament and well-crafted elaboration characterized urban housing for the upper middle class. Such neighborhoods are not to be found in profusion, either.

Those trying to maintain these integrated neighborhoods must fend off groups that see their efforts to attract new white residents as discrimination (which it is, in the strict sense) and as a way to drive the poor out of these urban neighborhoods. What one learns from such neighborhood stories is that the effort to maintain integration must be just that, an effort, without assured success.

If an area is located far from expanding black areas, if the values of its properties are high, integration does not necessarily mean increasing fear of crime, value decline, and neighborhood deterioration. There are hundreds of such areas, unremarked on and unrecorded in the socio- logical literature, and it is inevitable there will be more as the black mid- dle class expands. Richard Nathan of the Nelson A. Rockefeller Institute of Government is now studying them; his studies will reduce the domi- nant tendency to emphasize problems and may demonstrate how peo- ple with some resources following their interests naturally produce integration, the effect I expected twenty-five years ago. The environment of civil rights laws, increasing opportunity and achievement for many blacks, and the change to more tolerant attitudes have had their effect. The numbers of black families living in integrated circumstances, though, is apparently relatively small, for the expansion of such areas makes no substantial impact on Massey and Denton's measures. They show a glacial rate of decline in segregation and isolation, though they mark some success in the integration of African Americans into American society.

Attention, however, is concentrated for good reason on the isolation of the black poor. The persistence of this black ghetto tells us that the black of today is, whatever the cause, not the immigrant of yesterday or even the immigrant of today, who is less segregated and isolated than American blacks. The isolation of the black poor reflects a profound divide in American society. The prognosis is hardly encouraging. The leading candidate in the field of activist policy at the moment is the Gautreaux program in Chicago. Following lawsuits attacking racial iso- lation in Chicago's public housing projects, lawsuits that went to the Supreme Court, a program has been implemented by the Department of Housing and Urban Development in which five thousand low-income families have been relocated into white suburban areas.[24] It seems suc- cessful, as measured by the ability to find suburban landlords who would accept subsidized inner-city, female-headed families, by the recruitment of such families to make the move, by the contentment of these families with their new houses and neighborhoods, and by the effects on the chil- dren's education. The success of a program on such a scale led Henry

Cisneros, while Secretary of Housing and Urban Development, to try to expand it, but that expansion is hostage to the fate of appropriations for the heavy housing subsidies that are required by the program.

In the end, whatever the good of the Gautreaux program, one is doubtful about its effects in bringing black and white together. Its scale can never match the huge size of the inner-city black ghettoes. Perhaps more important, it aims at bringing together the black poor and the generally nonworking poor in subsidized apartments and houses with the nonblack working and middle class. That is trying to do too much. In 1973 that indefatigable proponent of measures to advance integration, Anthony Downs, coined a subtle phrase to describe a more reasonable objective: dispersed economic integration.[25] Downs meant to advise us that bringing together the races was hard enough without adding the further difficulty of bringing together the *classes*, something that the pattern of American urban development has never been good at doing. Our expectation has always been that the poor improve themselves by becoming less poor and then by moving to the neighborhoods of the less poor, leaving the ghetto behind.[26] They do not characteristically improve themselves by inserting themselves into areas they cannot afford before their economic circumstances have improved—or worse, to describe Gautreaux properly, by being inserted, through government subsidies, into areas they cannot afford. To the cultural differences of race, which are not insubstantial, are then added the cultural differences of class. To expect this to work, to take this as a model, is to demand too much.

One could tell a similar story about desegregation or racial integration of our schools. This effort has been frustrated primarily by the spatial separation of blacks and whites in our cities. If elementary public schools served the surrounding neighborhood, they inevitably were mostly black or white—segregated, in the current lexicon. The only way of changing this was busing, to which parents expressed enormous resistance, either through direct confrontation, as in Boston, or more commonly by withdrawing their children from public schools or moving to areas with schools unaffected by busing. The resistance was attacked as racist, and often was, but it was also a reflection of parents' concern over the education and environment of their children, who, as is often pointed out, only go through school once. The opposition to busing also reflected a widespread indignation over a degree of governmental intervention that most people believed went too far. Busing was instituted in a large number of American cities, but with the increase of black school populations and the reduction in the white population of cities through suburbanization, it often became a futile exercise of moving black students from all-black schools to schools only marginally less black. Courts are now allowing cities to suspend busing for integration. We can tell success stories about busing, as we can about some efforts to integrate housing racially, but the successes have not affected the overall picture of separation.

If the schools were going to be all black or mostly black, and if their teachers and administrators changed to reflect in some degree the changing school population, it was the most natural thing in the world that some cognizance would be taken of the race and presumed distinctive experience of the children. This was being done in many places long before the term *multiculturalism* was applied to it. The ground for multiculturalism in its more extensive form was prepared by the continuing separation of black and white, which has become increasingly, with the rise of the Hispanic and Asian populations through immigration, the separation of black and nonblack. Mexican American and other Hispanic children are also highly concentrated in some schools, but we can attribute the concentration to the impact of immigration. It is not very different from the overwhelming Jewish or Italian schools of the age of mass immigration and will last as long as immigration remains at a high level. The facts of declining residential separation and increasing intermarriage of second- and third-generation Hispanics tell us clearly that their degree of concentration is a first- and second-generation immigrant phenomenon. It is not the same story as the concentration or separation of blacks, which has been maintained for more than a century since they were freed from slavery.

Government has been as ineffective in overcoming segregation at the elementary school level as it has been in overcoming the prevailing residential segregation, though government programs have tried to do so. Government action can never match, in scale and impact, the crescive effects of individual, voluntary decisions. This has raised group after group in the past and is breaking down the barriers of ethnicity and race today, but these effects have operated excruciatingly slowly when it comes to American blacks. They have operated to some extent, as we see by the greatly expanded number of blacks making middle-class incomes and by the creation of integrated middle-class neighborhoods. It is the rate of movement toward integration and the contrast with the patterns of immigrant groups that have been so disappointing. Why our expectations were so disappointed is still obscure, and all the research does not make it clearer. We have to go back to such factors as the disaster that encompassed the black family, the failure to close educational achievement gaps, the rise of worklessness among black males, and the increase in crime. Behind all these are other factors in infinite regress, among them prejudice and discrimination, which while declining are still evident.

This failure leads many to propose larger-scale governmental action, unlikely as the prospects for such are in the present and foreseeable political climate. Even if that climate were better, it is hard to see what government programs could achieve. They would be opposed by the strongest motives that move men and women: their concern for family, children, and property. A greater measure of government effort to directly promote residential integration and school integration is not the answer. The forces that will produce the changes we are looking for are individual and voluntaristic, rather than governmental and authoritative. To adapt the title of Glenn Loury's book, it will have to be one by one, individual by individual, family by family, neighborhood by neighborhood.[27] Slowly as these work, there is really no alternative.

Notes

1. Karl Taeuber and Alma Taeuber, *Negroes in Cities* (Aldine, 1965).

2. Anthony Downs, *Opening Up the Suburbs: An Urban Strategy for America* (Yale University Press, 1973).

3. Nathan Glazer, *Affirmative Discrimination* (Basic Books, 1975).

4. Ben Wattenberg and R. M. Scammon, "Black Progress and Liberal Rhetoric," *Commentary* 55 (1973), pp. 35–44.

5. Irving Kristol, "The Negro Today Is Like the Immigrant Yesterday," *New York Times Magazine*, September 11, 1966.

6. Nathan Glazer and Daniel P. Moynihan, *Beyond the Melting Pot* (MIT Press, 1963).

7. Samuel Lubell, *The Future of American Politics* (Harper and Bros., 1952).

8. Douglas S. Massey and Nancy A. Denton, *American Apartheid: Segregation and the Making of the Underclass* (Harvard University Press, 1993).

9. Ibid., p. 63.

10. The quotations that follow are from ibid., pp. 32, 66, 67, 86, 91.

11. Thomas Schelling, "On the Ecology of Micomotives," *Public Interest* 25 (1971), pp. 59–98.

12. For example, Jonathan Rieder, *Canarsie: The Jews and Italians of Brooklyn against Liberalism* (Harvard University Press, 1985).

13. Richard P. Taub, D. Garth Taylor, and Jan D. Dunham, *Paths of Neighborhood Change: Race and Crime in Urban America* (University of Chicago Press, 1984), pp. 113–18, 135, 136.

14. David M. Cutler and Edward L. L. Glaeser, "Are Ghettoes Good or Bad?" (Harvard University and National Bureau for Economic Research, 1995).

15. William Labov and Wendell A. Harris, "De Facto Segregation of Black and White Vernaculars," in *Diversity and Diachrony*, edited by David Sankoff (Amsterdam: John Benjamins, 1986), pp. 17–18.

16. Paul Farhi, "A Television Trend: Audiences in Black and White," *Washington Post*, November 29, 1994.

17. Massey and Denton, *American Apartheid*, pp. 63–65.

18. Jennifer L. Hochschild, *Facing Up to the American Dream: Race, Class, and the Soul of the Nation* (Princeton University Press, 1995), p. 152.

19. See David L. Kirp, John P. Dwyer, and Larry A. Rosenthal, *Our Town: Race, Housing, and the Soul of Suburbia* (Rutgers University Press, 1995); Charles M. Haar, *Suburbs under Siege: Race, Space, and Audacious Judges* (Princeton University Press, 1996).

20. Harold Husock, "Subsidizing Discrimination at Starrett City," *City Journal* 2, no. 1 (1992), pp. 48–53.

21. Hillel Levine and Lawrence Harmon, *The Death of an American Jewish Community: A Tragedy of Good Intentions* (Free Press, 1992).

22. Taub, Taylor, and Dunham, *Paths of Neighborhood Change*.

23. Andrew Wiese, "Neighborhood Diversity: Social Change, Ambiguity, and Fair Housing," *Journal of Urban Affairs* 17 (1995), pp. 107–30.

24. J. Rosenbaum and others, "Can the Kerner Commission's Housing Strategy Improve Employment, Education, and Social Integration for Low-Income Blacks?" *North Carolina Law Review* 71 (1993), pp. 1519–56; Leonard S. Rubinowitz, "Metropolitan Public Housing Desegregation Remedies: Chicago's Privatization Program," *Northern Illinois University Law Review* 12 (1992), pp. 589–669.

25. Downs, *Opening Up the Suburbs*, chapter 12.

26. Harold Husock, "A Critique of Mixed Income Housing," *Responsive Community* 5 (1995), pp. 34–49.

27. Glenn Loury, *One by One, from the Inside Out: Essays and Reviews on Race and Responsibility in America* (Free Press, 1995).

ten

Black Churches and the Inner-City Poor

John J. Dilulio Jr.

Under what, if any, conditions can the life prospects of today's black inner-city poor be improved—and how, if at all, can we foster those conditions? Supporting black churches and other faith-based grassroots organizations performing youth and community outreach functions in poor inner-city neighborhoods is necessary and vital (but insufficient) for repairing the social fabric and restoring economic vitality in truly disadvantaged urban black neighborhoods. This is especially true for those clergy, volunteers, and persons of faith at the street level, who are doing the most to monitor, mentor, and minister to the daily needs of inner-city black children. Such persons strive to help these children, from innocent toddlers to pregnant teenagers and young males on probation, to avoid violence, achieve literacy, access jobs, and otherwise reach adulthood physically, educationally, and economically whole.

As I caution elsewhere, religious institutions alone cannot cure America's social and civic ills, including the social problems that disproportionately afflict the black inner-city poor.[1] It remains to be seen how, if at all, local faith-based efforts can be taken to scale in ways that predictably, reliably, and cost-effectively cut crime, reduce poverty, or yield other desirable social consequences. Still, overlooking, unduly discounting, or simply failing to support the outreach efforts of black churches and other inner-city faith communities is the single biggest mistake that can be made by anyone who cares about those who call the inner cities home.

Fortunately, it is a mistake that is becoming somewhat less common, even in elite intellectual and policy circles, both left and right. "Now both [left and right] are beginning to form an unlikely alliance founded on the idea that the only way to rescue [inner-city] kids from the seductions of the drugs and gang cultures is with another, more powerful set of values," according to a *Newsweek* cover story. "And the only institution with the spiritual message and the physical presence to offer those traditional values, these strange bedfellows have concluded, is the church."[2]

This hopeful conclusion rests upon a constellation of ideas and findings: the relationship between religiosity and volunteerism in contemporary America; religious faith as a factor in ameliorating social problems; adult supports and structured activities for at-risk urban youth; the tradition of black churches as engines of youth and community outreach; surveys of the extent of church-anchored outreach in black urban neighborhoods; and the need for an action-oriented dialogue about race that focuses on black-white religious racial reconciliation and the needs of the black inner-city poor.

Black Inner-City Poverty

It is incontestable that black Americans have progressed economically over the last half-century.[3] Even analysts who emphasize the persistence of black poverty and black-white income gaps acknowledge that "there have been significant improvements since 1940 in the absolute and relative positions of blacks," that black Americans represent a trillion-dollar-plus annual market larger than that of "most countries in the world," and that "the majority of working-class and middle-class black families have made some important gains."[4] Moreover, black economic progress has clearly been accompanied by residential desegregation and substantial improvements in race relations. According to surveys by the Gallup Organization, white racial prejudice has steeply declined in the past several decades. Most blacks do not live in mostly or all black neighborhoods. Comparably matched groups of highly educated, higher income whites and blacks are equally satisfied with major aspects of their own everyday lives.[5]

While according to Gallup blacks remain substantially less likely than whites to perceive equality of treatment in housing, education, and other areas and substantially more likely than whites to favor affirmative action, research by Carol Swain and Bernard Silverman indicates that "whites and blacks are not separated by unbridgeable gaps." For example, whites and blacks "show surprising agreement on the allocation of educational opportunities in zero-sum situations where only one person can win," and harbor "similar ideas about fairness and justice in college admissions."[6]

The triumph of overall black economic progress and the narrowing of black-white differences on social issues cannot obscure the tragedy of black poverty and joblessness.[7] In 1978, William Julius Wilson published his analysis of "the declining significance of race," followed in 1987 by his treatise on the inner city's underclass and in 1996 by his study of inner-city joblessness.[8] Wilson's research reminds us that working-class and low-income blacks are hit especially hard when economic booms go bust. Black Americans made substantial economic progress in the 1960s, but each post-1970 recession exacted a disproportionate toll on blacks regardless of family structure. Robert B. Hill estimates that the four recessions between 1970 and 1985 led to a tripling in the jobless rates among blacks in two-parent families as well as among blacks in mother-only households.[9] As the national economy improved in the late 1980s, black men and women still had unemployment rates more than double those of whites. Even amid the boom years of the 1990s, more than 40 percent of black children, concentrated heavily in central city neighborhoods, continued to live in households below the poverty line. According to a recent study by Scott J. South and Kyle D. Crowder, despite unprecedented residential mobility, blacks remain substantially less likely than whites to escape high-poverty neighborhoods and considerably more likely to move into them.[10]

Millions of black children, through absolutely no fault of their own, remain economically disadvantaged in neighborhoods where jobs are few and where drugs, crime, and failed public schools are common. No one—at least no one who has actually spent time in such neighborhoods as North Central Philadelphia or South Central Los Angeles—can fail to acknowledge the plight of these children. Thus while the glass of black socioeconomic progress has become indisputably full for millions of middle- and upper middle-class blacks, it has remained more than half empty for those remaining in black inner-city neighborhoods.

Black Inner-City Crime

Just as some conservatives seem disposed to trivialize or deny the reality of inner-city black poverty, some liberals seem determined to minimize or deny the reality of black inner-city crime and to insist that high rates of black-on-black violence and black incarceration are mainly or solely a function of low incomes and racist policies rather than such risk factors as fatherlessness and child abuse. As growing numbers of black church leaders and others seem disposed to argue, however, although poverty and racism are undoubtedly among the so-called root causes of black inner-city crime, they are hardly its sole determinants, and they alone cannot begin to explain differences in crime rates and incarceration rates between blacks and whites, differences in these rates among blacks, or the 1985 to 1995 epidemic of black male youth violence.

In the mid-1990s blacks were roughly 12 percent of the total U.S. residential population. According to the Uniform Crime Reports of the Federal Bureau of Investigation, blacks committed about 40 percent of all weapons violations, 42 percent of all rapes, 54 percent of all murders, 59 percent of all robberies, and 42 percent of all violent crimes.[11] According to James Alan Fox, black males ages fourteen to twenty-four were slightly over 1 percent of the total U.S. residential population but 17 percent of the homicide victims and 30 percent of the murderers.[12]

It has been widely and accurately reported that in the mid-1990s about a third of blacks males in their twenties were under correctional supervision on any given day (in prison, in jail, on probation, or on parole).[13] In 1997, the U.S. Bureau of Justice Statistics calculated that a black male had about a 29 percent lifetime likelihood of going to prison, compared to a 4 percent lifetime likelihood of imprisonment for white males.[14]

In 1996, about 29 percent of black households, versus 14 percent of white households, were below the official poverty line ($16,036 for a family of four). The former figure was the lowest proportion of blacks living below the poverty line since the U.S. Census Bureau began keeping such statistics in 1955. A socially and morally unacceptable four in ten black children lived in homes below the poverty line in the mid-1990s. Still, since the mid-1970s rates of childhood poverty among blacks and many other indexes of black economic distress, even in inner-city neighborhoods, remained unchanged or improved while rates of black youth crime and delinquency remained high or soared higher.[15]

Despite much conventional wisdom to the contrary, most prisoners, black and white, were gainfully employed at some point before their most recent conviction or incarceration, while many had legitimate jobs during the period that they did the crime or crimes that resulted in their most recent trouble with the law.[16] If anything, therefore, the worsening of black inner-city crime during years of relative and absolute gains in material well-being is an acute case of what UCLA's James Q. Wilson described as the paradox of "crime amidst plenty."[17]

As Glenn Loury reasons, the "simple fact of poverty is surely not an adequate explanation" for the "extraordinary disparity" in black and white crime rates.[18] By the same token, racial discrimination is not an adequate explanation for the extraordinary disparity in black and white incarceration rates. According to a 1998 report prepared by the Council of Economic Advisers for the President's Initiative on Race, "Research suggests that most or all of the differences in the likelihood of conviction and imprisonment can be explained" by factors other than racial discrimination, "such as severity of crime or prior record of the offender."[19]

Even if one believes that racism and poverty are the twin determinants of black crime and incarceration rates, it still makes sense to ponder risk factors along with root causes. Among the social risk factors that go the longest way toward accounting not only for the difference between black and white rates of crime and incarceration but also for the differences in these rates among blacks are those that relate to the densities of loving, capable, responsible adults in the daily lives of children and young adults. Two such interrelated risk factors are the absence of fathers and child abuse. In 1993, 69 percent of births to black mothers, versus 24 percent of births to white mothers, were out of wedlock. In 1994, 96 percent of black teen births, versus 67 percent of white teen births, were out of wedlock. In 1996, 53 percent of black children, versus 19 percent of white children, lived in mother-only homes.

Robin Karr-Morse and Meredith Wiley observe that research on

the roles of African American and Hispanic fathers in their children's development has been sparse. But the data that do exist on African-American men are particularly troubling. . . . Where fathers have never married the mothers, 57 percent consistently visit their children in the first two years. But by the time the children are 7.5 years old, fewer than 25 percent of fathers are consistently visiting their children. The lack of a father's presence has a direct impact on the child.[20]

Indeed it does. As indicated by a 1993 analysis by June O'Neill and Anne Hill, the likelihood that a young male will commit crime doubles if he is raised without a father and triples if he lives in a neighborhood with a high concentration of mother-only homes, such that black males raised in public housing in mother-only welfare-dependent homes are about twice as likely to commit crimes as otherwise comparable black males raised with a father but also on welfare and in public housing.[21] Likewise, as reported in a 1998 study by Cynthia Harper and Sara McLanahan, even after controlling for race, income, and other socioeconomic variables, fatherless boys are twice as likely as boys living in two-parent homes to be incarcerated, and each year spent in a fatherless home raises a boy's odds of being imprisoned by about 5 percent.[22]

With regard to race, the criminogenic influence of fatherlessness can manifest itself in many ways, the most direct and obvious of which is captured in the classic 1965 statement of the problem by Daniel Patrick Moynihan: "A community that allows a large number of young men to grow up in broken families, dominated by women, never acquiring any stable relationship to male authority . . . asks for and gets chaos."[23]

Boys without loving, law-abiding fathers to actively monitor and mentor them on a daily basis are more likely to act out at home and in school, run wild on the streets, and get into trouble with the law. If much of the relevant post-1985 empirical research is any guide, boys without such fathers are also more likely to be severely maltreated at home by one or both of their biological parents, or by a biological mother's boyfriend, in ways that increase their incidence of future crime and delinquency.

There is growing evidence of a nexus consisting of child abuse, fatherlessness, and crime. The results of a major longitudinal study as reported by the National Institute of Justice in 1992 indicate that abuse of children increases their chances of future delinquency and crime by about 40 percent.[24] A 1992 study by Leslie Margolin indicates that in mother-only homes the mother's live-in boyfriends provide almost no nonparental child care but are responsible for nearly two-thirds of all nonparental child abuse.[25] In a 1995 study, Carolyn Smith and Terrance Thornberry analyze data indicating that only 3 percent of children raised by both parents, versus 19 percent of those raised by cohabitating partners and other adults, are abused; in a second 1995 study, Smith notes that child abuse "has long been associated with problematic outcomes for children," including criminality.[26] Or, in the 1995 words of Mark Fleisher, the country's leading urban street crime ethnographer, an "abundance of scholarly evidence shows that anti-social and delinquent tendencies emerge early in the lives of neglected, abused, and unloved youngsters, often by age nine."[27]

I agree with the University of Southern California's Susan Estrich when she writes that "the only way truly to address racism in the criminal justice system is to cut the crime rate among blacks—to try to inoculate the children even as we punish many of their fathers and brothers. It is what we would do if it were our white sons facing their future." It is not racist to lock up violent and habitual criminals. "But planning prisons for preschoolers is" racist.[28]

The good news is that many clergy and religious volunteers, both black and white, concur that we must aggressively reach all socially at-risk preschoolers with loving, caring adults; reconnect responsible young fathers on probation and behind bars with their children and families; and build churches, not jails.

Religiosity and Volunteers

How we approach black inner-city poverty and crime is bound to be affected by religious ideals, influences, and institutions. From Alexis de Tocqueville to the latest social science findings, it is abundantly clear that "the United States is one of the most devout nations of the entire industrialized world, in terms of religious beliefs and practices."[29] Belief in God remains the norm in America, with levels of belief ranging between 94 percent and 99 percent over the past five decades.

Black Americans are in many ways the most religious people in America. Some 82 percent of blacks (versus 67 percent of whites) are church members; 82 percent of blacks (versus 55 percent of whites) say that religion is "very important in their life"; and 86 percent of blacks (versus 60 percent of whites) believe that religion "can answer all or most of today's problems."[30]

All reports of the death of organized religion and religious sentiment in America have been greatly exaggerated. Since the end of the Second World War, we have witnessed what Roger Finke and Rodney Clark aptly describe as the "churching of America," resulting by the mid-1990s in a nation with an estimated half a million churches, temples, and mosques, two thousand or more religious denominations, and an unknown number of independent churches.[31] In 1995 Gallup's religion index, an ongoing measurement of eight key religious beliefs and practices of the American public, hit a ten-year high.[32]

Laws have grown more faith-friendly. For example, the federal government's latest welfare reform overhaul measure, the Personal Responsibility and Work Opportunity Reconciliation Act of 1996, contains section 104, the so-called charitable choice provision. This provision encourages states to utilize "faith-based organizations in serving the poor and needy"; requires that religious organizations be permitted to receive contracts, vouchers, and other government funding on the same basis as any other nongovernmental provider; and protects "the religious integrity and character of faith-based organizations that are willing to accept government funds."[33] Charitable choice covers the major federal antipoverty and social welfare programs (temporary assistance to needy families, medicaid, supplemental security income, food stamps), and

Congress could expand it to juvenile justice programs and other policy domains. Many states, most notably Texas, have moved aggressively to reorient their antipoverty programs around charitable choice and kindred state laws favoring church-state cooperation.[34]

Philanthropy, too, has been gradually tilting toward religion. In 1996 three foundations with long-standing programs in religion, the Lilly Endowment, the Pew Charitable Trusts, and the James Irvine Foundation, made record religion grants of $60 million, $13 million, and $7.7 million, respectively. In 1997, the Robert Wood Johnson Foundation made its eight hundredth $25,000 grant to its Faith in Action program, which mobilizes interfaith networks of religious volunteers to serve some 200,000 elderly and disabled Americans. The program's director describes it as "the first mega program undertaken" by the foundation and "the largest project" in the foundation's history.[35]

It is hardly surprising that networks of interfaith volunteers are the backbone of such a program. As Andrew Greely aptly summarizes the evidence, "frequency of church attendance and membership in church organizations correlate strongly with voluntary service. People who attend services once a week or more are approximately twice as likely to volunteer as those who attend rarely if ever." Furthermore, religious organizations and "relationships related to their religion" appear to be the major forces in mobilizing volunteers in America. Even a third of purely secular volunteers (persons who did not volunteer for specifically religious activities) also relate their service "to the influence of a relationship based in their religion."[36] According to Gallup,

churches and other religious bodies are the major supporters of voluntary services for neighborhoods and communities. Members of a church or synagogue . . . tend to be much more involved in charitable activity, particularly through organized groups. Almost half of the church members did unpaid volunteer work in a given year, compared to only a third of non-members. . . . Religion would appear to have an early impact upon volunteers and charitable giving. . . . Among the 76 percent of teens who reported that they were members of religious institutions, 62 percent were also volunteers, and 56 percent were charitable contributors. By contrast, among those who reported no religious affiliation, far fewer were either volunteers (44 percent) or contributors (25 percent).[37]

Faith Factor Findings

Is there any scientific evidence to show that religious do-gooding does any good or to justify the faith of most black Americans that religion can "answer all or most of today's problems"? Over the last several years, journalists seem to have become more interested in this question, often crediting the ministry with working cooperatively with police and probation officials, working one-on-one with the city's most severely at-risk youngsters, and thereby helping to engineer a dramatic drop in youth crime and the virtual elimination of gun-related youth homicides. Two months before the *Newsweek* cover story featuring Boston's Reverend Eugene Rivers, *Time* featured "In the Line of Fire," the tale of Brother Bill, a Catholic lay worker who "repeatedly walks into gunfire to stop the shooting—and love the unloved."[38] Two years earlier, the cover of *US News & World Report* asked "Can Churches Cure America's Social Ills?" The story answered largely in the affirmative.[39]

While such faith factor journalism is out ahead of the empirical research on religion and social action, it is hardly pure hype. As UCLA's James Q. Wilson succinctly summarizes the small but not insignificant body of credible evidence to date, "religion, independent of social class, reduces deviance."[40] David Larson pioneered inquiry into the influence of the faith factor on public health outcomes, research that led to new training programs at Harvard and three dozen other medical schools. In more recent work with criminologist Byron Johnson, Larson reviews some four hundred juvenile delinquency studies published between 1980 and 1997. They find that the better the study design and measurement methodology, the greater the likelihood the research will find statistically significant and beneficial results associated with the faith factor. The more scientific the study, the more optimistic are its findings about the extent to which "religion reduces deviance." A 1997 study by Larson and Johnson finds that prisoners who participate in Bible studies behind bars are only a third as likely to be rearrested a year after being released than otherwise comparable prisoners who do not participate in Bible studies before being paroled.[41]

In another major review of the relevant research literature, David Evans and his associates confirm that the religiosity and crime relationship for adults is neither spurious nor contingent. "Religion, as indicated by religious activities, had direct personal effects on adult criminality as measured by a broad range of criminal acts. Further, the relationship held even with the introduction of secular controls."[42] In other words, religion matters in reducing adult crime. Beyond crime and delinquency, in a sprightly 1996 synopsis of various faith factor research, Patrick Fagan of the Heritage Foundation summarizes studies suggesting that religion enhances family stability (the family that prays together is indeed more likely to stay together), improves health, reduces adolescent sexual activities and teenage pregnancies, cuts alcohol and drug abuse, and reinforces other measures of social stability.[43]

In relation to black inner-city poverty and related social ills, perhaps the single most illustrative line of religion-reduces-deviance research begins with a 1985 study by Harvard economist Richard Freeman, runs through the work of Larson and Johnson, and continues through the community development, mentoring, and faith factor research of analysts at Public/Private Ventures (P/PV), a Philadelphia-based national nonprofit youth policy research organization. In 1985, Freeman reported that churchgoing, independent of other factors, made young black males from high-poverty neighborhoods substantially more likely to escape poverty, crime, and other social ills.[44] In their reanalysis and extension of Freeman's work, Larson and Johnson mine national longitudinal data on urban black youth and find that, using a more multidimensional measure of religious commitment than churchgoing, religion is indeed a powerful predictor of escaping poverty, crime, and other social ills, more powerful even than such variables as peer influences.[45] Like Freeman, Larson and Johnson conjecture that the potential of churchgoing and other religious influences to improve the life prospects of poor black urban youth is in part a function of how churchgoing and other faith factors influence how young people spend their time, the extent of their engagement in positive structured activities, and the degree to which they are supported by responsible adults.

Support for Youth

This conjecture is borne out in part by an important 1998 P/PV analysis, based on original survey and field research, of how predominantly minority, low-income urban youth spend their time in the moderately poor neighborhoods of three cities: Austin, Texas; Savannah, Georgia; and St. Petersburg, Florida. As P/PV researchers Cynthia Sipe and Patricia Ma observe, much has "been written on adolescents' use of their discretionary time and the lack of positive activities to fill that time. Many youth fall prey to antisocial activities in good part because positive activities and safe places are not available at crucial times" and during "so-called gap periods" (after school, weekends, summers).[46] Sipe and Ma analyze data on how three different cohorts of youth (twelve-to-fourteen-year-olds, fifteen-to-seventeen-year-olds, and eighteen-to-twenty-year-olds) spend their after-school time across the neighborhoods of three cities.

First, the bad news. A majority of youth in each cohort, neighborhood, and city spent most of their after-school time just "hanging out," on "unstructured leisure," or on things other than homework, chores, jobs, and so on.[47] Overall, "a disturbingly high share" (from 15 to 25 percent) of youth were "not engaged in any positive structured activities," had "no or very few adults in their lives," and were "not working."[48]

Now, however, the good news. Across all groups and cities, most youth who did receive adult support and guidance (whether at home, in school, or via community organizations) and did participate in positive structured activities were significantly more likely than their disconnected peers to succeed: "Youth who are engaged in more activities, have more leadership experiences and more adult support also tend to have higher self-efficacy, better grades and be less involved in risk activity," including but not limited to less "delinquency and gang involvement."[49]

Finally, the good news about religion. P/PV's youth study was undertaken as part of a larger, six-city, resident-driven project launched in 1993 and known as Community Change for Youth Development (CCYD).[50] Those who designed CCYD, including P/PV President Gary Walker, expected to find that public schools and programs like Boys Clubs, Girls Clubs, Police Athletic League, Ys, and Big Brothers Big Sisters provide substantial and beneficial support for youth in these disadvantaged communities. They were not entirely disappointed; but they also found something that they did not expect or set out to find, namely, churches and faith-based programs serving as after-school safe havens and playing a major support for youth role (recreation, mentoring, child care, meals, and more) in these neighborhoods.

For example, in the predominantly Latino Austin study site, twenty-four churches sponsored various programs for the community, and over half of the youth participated in local religious services. In the Savannah study site, fifty-two churches dwarfed schools both in sheer numbers and in terms of outreach programs and activities for neighborhood youth, 97 percent of them black. And the surprising strength of churches in the St. Petersburg study site was ratified, as it were, by the fact that P/PV held its 1998 CCYD conference there and featured none other than Boston's Reverend Rivers as the keynote speaker. Indeed, from 1996 to 1998, P/PV's CCYD experience, and a fresh look at the implications of its own research on mentoring, led the organization to develop a new research program on religion and at-risk youth.

For years, P/PV led in the production and dissemination of evaluation research on mentoring programs.[51] To date, the most widely publicized P/PV study of mentoring is its 1995 evaluation of the Big Brothers Big Sisters of America program. P/PV researchers Joseph Tierney and Jean Baldwin Grossman report that youth (most of them low-income minority youth) who were matched with a Big Brother or Sister reaped significant benefits, compared with their counterparts who remained on agency waiting lists.[52] The Littles were 46 percent less likely to initiate drug use and 27 percent less likely to initiate alcohol use. They were about a third less likely to hit someone. They skipped school half as many days as wait-listed youth. They also liked school more, got slightly better grades, and formed more positive relationships with their parents and peers. These effects held for both boys and girls across all races. The study received lots of positive public notice, elicited bipartisan endorsements from national leaders, and was invoked repeatedly at the 1996 presidential volunteer summit in Philadelphia led by Colin Powell.

There were, however, at least two clouds in the study's silver lining. The study was possible only because thousands of eligible children remained on waiting lists. Worse, even if there were adult volunteers aplenty, the inner-city youth who needed responsible nonparental adult support and guidance in their lives would be least likely to get it. The simple reason is that Big Brothers Big Sisters, and most other effective mentoring programs that reach at-risk urban youth, presupposes a youth who already has at least one parent, legal guardian, or other responsible adult in his or her life, an adult who is caring and functional enough to sign them up, follow through on interviews and phone calls, fill out forms, and so forth.

Many low-income minority youth lack even that much social capital. Recall the CCYD youth study's disturbing finding that anywhere from 15 to 25 percent of minority youth in "moderately poor" neighborhoods were completely or totally "disconnected." There is every reason to suppose that the unsupported fraction runs even higher in the poorest inner-city neighborhoods, places that contribute disproportionately to such grim social statistics as the following: each year since 1993 there have been roughly one million substantiated cases of child abuse and neglect; about 1.3 million persons age eighteen or younger have one or both parents in prison or jail; more than 70 percent of all black births are out of wedlock; by age eight, three-quarters of nonmarital black children have no regular contact with their biological fathers; and, sadly, so on.

"Most private, nonprofit mentoring programs," comments P/PV's Walker, a twenty-five year veteran of the field, "like most social policy-driven youth development programs, simply don't reach or support the most severely at-risk inner-city youth."[53]

Black Church Outreach, an Alive Tradition

The black church's uniquely powerful community outreach tradition is grounded in eight major historically black Christian churches: African Methodist Episcopal, African Methodist Episcopal Zion, Christian

Methodist Episcopal, Church of God in Christ, National Baptist Convention of America, National Baptist Convention, USA, National Missionary Baptist Convention, and the Progressive National Baptist Convention. There are also scores of independent or quasi-independent black churches or church networks and at least nine certified religious training programs operated by accredited seminaries that are directed toward ministry in black churches and black faith communities. The eight major black denominations alone encompass some 65,000 churches and about 20 million members.

Unfortunately, until quite recently, that outreach tradition and what it portends for social action against inner-city ills has been largely ignored by a strange bedfellows assortment of academics and intellectual elites. Until the 1990s, for example, the richly religious lives of black Americans and the black church outreach tradition were given short shrift by both historians and social scientists—and not just by white historians and social scientists. In the *National Journal of Sociology*, Andrew Billingsley, the dean of black family studies, notes that the subject was largely ignored even by leading black scholars who were keenly aware of "the social significance of the black church," including many who "were actually members of a black church."[54]

For example, James Blackwell's 1975 book *The Black Community*, considered by Billingsley and several other experts to be "the best study" of its kind since W. E. B. Du Bois's 1899 classic, *The Philadelphia Negro*, devoted not a single chapter to the black church; and Billingsley's own 1968 book, *Black Families in White America*, written as a rebuttal to the 1965 Moynihan Report, "devoted less than two pages to discussing the relevance of the black church as a support system for African-American families." Billingsley speculates that black intellectuals ignore black churches in part out of a false fidelity to the canons of objective scholarship.

A refined and empirically well-grounded perspective on variations in the extent of black church outreach is provided by sociologist Harold Dean Trulear, an ordained black minister who did outreach work in New Jersey, taught for eight years at the New York Theological Seminary, conducted extensive research on black clergy training, and is vice president for research on religion and at-risk youth at P/PV:

When it comes to youth and community outreach in the inner city, not all black urban churches are created equal. . . . Naturally, it's in part a function of high resident membership. Inner-city churches with high resident membership cater more to high-risk neighborhood youth than . . . black churches with inner-city addresses but increasingly or predominantly suburbanized or commuting congregations. . . . [The high resident membership black churches] tend to cluster by size and evangelical orientation. . . . It's the small and medium-sized churches . . . [especially] the so-called . . . blessing stations and specialized youth chapels with their charismatic leader and their small, dedicated staff of adult volunteers [that] . . . do a disproportionate amount of the up-close and personal outreach work with the worst off inner-city youth.[55]

Today, a number of intellectual and policy leaders are reclaiming the black church tradition. In a 1997 essay, Boston University economists Glenn Loury and Linda Datcher Loury argue persuasively that a "spirit of self-help, rooted in a deep-seated sense of self-respect, was widely embraced among blacks of all ideological persuasions well into this century." They rebut the view that "economic factors ultimately drive" behavioral problems "involving sexuality, marriage, childbearing, and parenting" and challenge the notion that merely fiddling with economic incentives via policy changes can change behavior for the good. Rather, they argue, voluntary associations, "as exemplified by religious institutions," can be valuable allies in the battle against social pathology.[56] From a less academic, more practice-driven perspective, Robert L. Woodson Sr., president of the National Center for Neighborhood Enterprise in Washington, D.C., reclaims the black church outreach tradition in his 1998 book on how "today's community healers are reviving our streets and neighborhoods."[57]

Surveys of Church-Based Outreach

How common are black-led outreach ministries? What, if any, systematic evidence suggests that the extent of youth and community outreach by black churches is nontrivial? As Harold Dean Trulear observes, "Simply stated, there has yet to be a survey of the blessing stations and youth chapels that do most of the actual work with the worst-off kids in black inner-city neighborhoods." Still, the pathbreaking research of scholars such as Eric C. Lincoln and Lawrence H. Mamiya, combined with recent systematic research by Trulear and others, should persuade even a dedicated skeptic to take black church-based outreach seriously.

In a recent study, P/PV's Jeremy White and Mary de Marcellus report on the results of their intensive six-month field exploration of youth-serving ministries in the District of Columbia.[58] They interviewed leaders and volunteers in 129 of the city's faith-based ministries, including on-site visits to 79 churches, faith-based nonprofit organizations, and schools, virtually all of them led by blacks and serving predominantly black populations. Based on this research, they conclude that "there is a critical mass of faith-based organizations in Washington, D.C., that work directly and intensively with at-risk youth." The programs fall into six major categories: after-school programs, tutoring programs, evangelization, gang violence prevention, youth groups, and mentoring. Interestingly, however, only 7 percent of the programs focus exclusively on the evangelization of children in the form of youth church, Bible study, or street preaching.

Although the language and motivations of most of the ministers and volunteers they studied are plainly spiritual and religious, none of the programs required youth to belong to a particular church, profess any particular religious beliefs, or agree to eventual "churching" as a condition for receiving services, entering church buildings, or otherwise benefiting from the programs. Likewise, almost none of the programs, even those that furnish children with material goods such as clothes or books, charge a fee. As one outreach minister phrases it: "The cost of real love is no charge."

The results of a survey of "faith-based service providers in the nation's capital" were published in 1998 by the Urban Institute.[59] The survey finds that 95 percent of the congregations perform outreach services. The 226 religious congregations (of 1,100 surveyed) that responded (67 of them in the District of Columbia, the rest in Maryland or Virginia) provided more than a thousand community services to more than

250,000 individuals in 1996. The services included food, clothing, and financial assistance. The survey was limited to religious congregations. Local faith-based nonprofit organizations were not surveyed.

In the mid-1990s a six-city survey of how more than a hundred randomly selected urban churches (and four synagogues) constructed in 1940 or earlier serve their communities was undertaken by Ram A. Cnnan of the University of Pennsylvania. The study was commissioned and published by Partners for Sacred Places, a Philadelphia-based national nonprofit organization dedicated to the care and good use of older religious properties.[60] Congregations were surveyed in Philadelphia, New York, Chicago, Indianapolis, Mobile, Alabama, and the Bay area (Oakland and San Francisco). Each church surveyed participated in a series of in-depth interviews.

Among the Cnnan-Partners survey's key findings were the following: 93 percent of the churches open their doors to the larger community; each church provides an average of at least 5,300 hours of volunteer support to its community programs (the equivalent of two and a half full-time volunteers stationed year-round at the church); each church provides an average of $140,000 a year in community programs, or about sixteen times what it receives from program beneficiaries; each church supports an average of four major programs and provides informal and impromptu services as well; and poor children who are not the sons or daughters of church members or otherwise affiliated with the church benefit from church-supported programs more than any other single group.

The best known and still the most comprehensive survey focusing exclusively on black churches was published in 1990 by Eric Lincoln and Lawrence Mamiya. In their book, *The Black Church in the African-American Experience,* they report on the results of surveys encompassing nearly 1,900 ministers and more than 2,100 churches.[61] Some 71 percent of black clergy reported that their churches engaged in community outreach programs, including day care, job search, substance abuse prevention, and food and clothing distribution. Black urban churches, the authors found, were generally more engaged in outreach than rural ones. While many urban churches also engaged in quasi-political activities and organizing, few received government money, and most clergy expressed concern about receiving government money. Only about 8 percent of all the churches surveyed received any federal government funds.

A number of site-specific and regional surveys of black churches followed the publication of Lincoln and Mamiya's book. So far all of them have been broadly consistent with the Lincoln-Mamiya survey results on black church outreach. To cite just two examples, in a survey of 150 black churches in Atlanta, Naomi Ward and her colleagues find that 131 of the churches are "actively engaged in extending themselves into the community." Likewise, a survey of 635 northern black churches finds that two-thirds of the churches engage in a wide range of "family-oriented community outreach programs," including mentoring, drug abuse prevention, teenage pregnancy prevention, and other outreach efforts "directed at children and youth."[62]

The raw data from the Lincoln-Mamiya surveys were reanalyzed in the course of a 1997 study of black theological education certificate programs (Bible institutes, denominational training programs, and seminary nondegree programs). The study was directed by Trulear in collaboration with Tony Carnes and commissioned by the Ford Foundation.[63] Trulear and Carnes report no problems with the Lincoln-Mamiya data. Rather, they compare certain of the Lincoln-Mamiya survey results to data gathered in their own survey of 724 students representing twenty-eight theological certificate programs that focus on serving black students. Again, the findings are quite consistent with those of the Lincoln-Mamiya study. For example, three-quarters of those surveyed by Trulear and Carnes report that their church encourages them "to be involved in my local community," more than half say that relevance to "my community's needs" is of major importance to them in choosing a theological certificate program, and about half are involved in certain types of charitable community work.

Religious Racial Reconciliation and the Poor

If black church outreach is so potent, why do inner-city poverty, crime, and other problems remain so severe? That is a fair question, but it can easily be turned around: How much worse would things be in Boston and Jamaica Queens, Philadelphia and Los Angeles and other cities were it not for the largely unsung efforts of faith-based youth and community outreach efforts? How much more would government or other charitable organizations need to expend, and how many volunteers would suddenly need to be mobilized, in the absence of church-anchored outreach? The only defensible answers are "much worse" and "lots," respectively.

Citizens who for whatever reasons are nervous about religion or enhanced church-state partnerships should focus on the consistent finding that faith-based outreach efforts benefit poor unchurched neighborhood children most of all. If these churches are so willing to support and reach out to "the least of these," surely they deserve the human and financial support of the rest us—corporations, foundations, and, where appropriate, government agencies.

The oldest racial divide in America has been, and continues to be, between blacks and whites. To be more specific, the divide is between black Christians and white Christians. Or, to be dangerously specific, it is between white and black Protestants who found themselves (or whose fathers and grandmothers found themselves) on opposite sides of the civil rights divide and, before that, Jim Crow. In recent years, though, I sense a thaw in relations between black and white Christians. Everywhere, it seems, new flowers of religious racial reconciliation and cooperation are starting to bud. Consider the Prison Fellowship Ministry, including its Neighbors Who Care program and its new initiative on children, youth, and families, designed to help provide outreach to the sons and daughters of incarcerated adults. Consider that the Catholic church has successfully provided excellent but affordable education to non-Catholic, low-income, inner-city minority children and has—as His Eminence Cardinal Bernard Law of Boston has done vis-à-vis the outreach ministry of Reverend Rivers and other local black Protestant clergy—supported black faith-based outreach efforts in other ways.

Along with Andrew Greely, I do not believe that churches or charity can or "should replace public support for those in distress."[64] Especially regarding social action to solve the problems of the black inner-city poor, I also agree with him that it is long past time to recognize that there are in America many more clergy and "religiously motivated volunteers than there are activists engaged in the culture wars," or, I might add, in debates about multiculturalism, political correctness, or other fashionable topics of elite ideological dispute.

I also agree with Father Richard John Neuhaus, who characterizes one of my earlier writings on black poverty as advancing the view that "religion is the key to anything good happening among the black poor" (well, at least the key to most good things that are happening among them).[65] I confess to being doubly in agreement with Father Neuhaus when he writes that, rather than turn our heads and harden our hearts to the plight of the black inner-city poor, rather than merely exposing "liberal fatuities about remedying the 'root causes' of poverty and crime . . . there must be another way. Just believing that is a prelude to doing something. The something in question is centered in religion that is both motive and means and extends to public policy tasks that should claim the attention of all Americans." Say amen.

Notes

1. John J. DiIulio Jr., "The Lord's Work: The Church and Civil Society," in *Community Works: The Revival of Civil Society in America,* edited by E. J. Dionne Jr. (Brookings, 1998), chapter 7.

2. John Leland, "Savior of the Streets," *Newsweek,* June 1, 1998, p. 22.

3. Stephan Thernstrom and Abigail Thernstrom, *America in Black and White: One Nation, Indivisible* (Simon and Schuster, 1997).

4. Quotations from, respectively, Gerald David Jaynes and Robin M. Williams Jr., eds., *A Common Destiny: Blacks and American Society* (National Academy Press, 1989), pp. 274; Marcus Alexis and Geraldine R. Henderson, "The Economic Base of African-American Communities: A Study of Consumption Patterns," in National Urban League, *The State of Black America, 1994* (1994), p. 81; Robert B. Hill and others, *Research on the African-American Family: A Holistic Perspective* (Westport, Conn.: Auburn House, 1993), p. 2.

5. Gallup Organization, *Black/White Relations in the United States, 1997* (Princeton, 1997).

6. Carol M. Swain and Bernard Silverman, "Where Blacks and Whites Agree," *Public Affairs Report, University of California, Berkeley* 39 (1998), pp. 8–9.

7. See John J. DiIulio Jr., "State of Grace," *National Review,* December 22, 1997, pp. 62–66.

8. William Julius Wilson, *The Declining Significance of Race* (University of Chicago Press, 1978); Wilson, *The Truly Disadvantaged: The Inner City, the Underclass, and Public Policy* (University of Chicago Press, 1987); Wilson, *When Work Disappears: The World of the New Urban Poor* (Knopf, 1996).

9. Robert B. Hill, "The Black Middle Class: Past, Present, and Future," in National Urban League, *The State of Black America, 1986* (1986), pp. 43–64.

10. Scott J. South and Kyle D. Crowder, "Escaping Distressed Neighborhoods: Individual, Community, and Metropolitan Influences," *American Journal of Sociology* 102 (1997), pp. 1040–84.

11. *Sourcebook of Criminal Justice Statistics* (Bureau of Justice Statistics, 1997), p. 384.

12. James Alan Fox, *Trends in Juvenile Violence* (Bureau of Justice Statistics, 1996), p. 1.

13. "A Shocking Look at Blacks and Crime," *US News & World Report,* October 16, 1995, p. 53.

14. *Lifetime Likelihood of Going to State or Federal Prison* (Bureau of Justice Statistics, 1997), p. 1.

15. Thernstrom and Thernstrom, *America in Black and White*; Thomas D. Boston and Catherine L. Ross, *The Inner City: Urban Poverty and Economic Development* (Transaction, 1997).

16. Anne Piehl, John Dilulio, and Bert Useem, *Right-Sizing Justice: Profiles of Prisoners in Three States* (Manhattan Institute, Center for Civic Innovation, 1999).

17. James Q. Wilson, *Thinking about Crime* (Basic Books, 1983), p. 13.

18. Glenn Loury. "Victims and Predators," *Times Literary Supplement,* September 25, 1995.

19. Council of Economic Advisers, *Changing America* (1999), p. 51.

20. Robin Karr-Morse and Meredith S. Wiley, *Ghosts from the Nursery: Tracing the Roots of Violence* (Atlantic Monthly Press, 1997), pp. 230–31.

21. June O'Neill and Anne M. Hill, "Underclass Behaviors in the United States" (City University of New York, Baruch College, 1993), summarized in Wade F. Horn, *Father Facts* (Gaithersburg, Md.: National Fatherhood Initiative, 1998), p. 61.

22. Cynthia C. Harper and Sara McLanahan, "Father Absence and Youth Incarceration," paper prepared for the annual meeting of the American Sociological Association, August 1998.

23. Daniel Patrick Moynihan, *The Negro Family: The Case for National Action,* reprinted in Lee Rainwater and William L. Yancy, *The Moynihan Report and the Politics of Controversy* (MIT Press, 1967).

24. National Institute of Justice, *Cycle of Violence* (1992).

25. Leslie Margolin, "Child Abuse by Mothers' Boyfriends," *Child Abuse and Neglect* (1992), pp. 541–51.

26. Carolyn Smith and Terrance Thornberry, "The Relationship between Childhood Maltreatment and Adolescent Involvement in Delinquency," *Criminology*

(1993), pp. 451–79; Carolyn Smith and others, "Resilient Youth: Identifying Factors That Prevent High-Risk Youth from Engaging in Delinquency and Drug Use," *Current Perspectives on Aging and the Life Cycle* (1995), p. 221.

27. Mark S. Fleisher, *Beggars and Thieves: Lives of Urban Street Criminals* (University of Wisconsin Press, 1995), p. 262.

28. Susan Estrich, *Getting Away with Murder: How Politics Is Destroying the Criminal Justice System* (Harvard University Press, 1998), p. 92.

29. George Gallup Jr., *Emerging Trends* 18 (Princeton Religion Research Center, March 1996), p. 5. Also see Richard Morin, "Keeping the Faith: A Survey Shows the United States Has the Most Churchgoing People in the Developed World," *Washington Post Weekly Edition,* January 12, 1998, p. 37.

30. George Gallup Jr., "Religion in America: Will the Vitality of Churches Be the Surprise of the Next Century?" *Public Perspective* (October-November 1995), p. 4.

31. Roger Finke and Rodney Stark, *The Churching of America, 1776–1990: Winners and Losers in Our Religious Economy* (Rutgers University Press, 1992).

32. Gallup, *Emerging Trends*, p. 1.

33. Center for Public Justice, *A Guide to Charitable Choice* (Washington, D.C.: 1997). Also see Carl H. Esbeck, "A Constitutional Case for Governmental Cooperation with Faith-Based Social Service Providers," *Emory Law Journal* 46 (1997), pp. 1–83; Stanley W. Carlson-Thies and James W. Skillen, eds., *Welfare in America: Christian Perspectives on a Policy in Crisis* (Cambridge, U.K.: Eerdmans, 1996).

34. For example, see Governor's Advisory Task Force on Faith-Based Community Service Groups, *Faith in Action: A New Vision for Church-State Cooperation in Texas* (State of Texas, 1996).

35. Mike Jackson, "Faith in Action Supporting Volunteering with 800 Grantees," *Advances: The Robert Wood Johnson Foundation Quarterly Newsletter* 1 (1998), p. 10.

36. Andrew Greely, "The Other Civic America: Religion and Social Capital," *American Prospect*, no. 32 (May-June 1997), pp. 70, 72.

37. Gallup, "Religion in America," p. 2.

38. Ron Stodghill II, "In the Line of Fire," *Time*, April 20, 1998, pp. 34–37.

39. Joseph P. Shapiro, "Can Churches Save America?" *US News & World Report*, September 9, 1996, pp. 46–53.

40. James Q. Wilson, "Two Nations," Francis Boyer lecture, American Enterprise Institute, December 4, 1997, p. 10.

41. David B. Larson and others, *Scientific Research on Spirituality and Health* (Radnor, Penn.: John M. Templeton Foundation, 1997); David B. Larson and Byron Johnson, *Religion: The Forgotten Factor in Cutting Youth Crime and Saving At-Risk Urban Youth* (Center for Civic Innovation and the Jeremiah Project, Manhattan Institute, 1998); David B. Larson and others, "Religion Programs, Institutional Adjustment, and Recidivism among Former Inmates in Prison Fellowship Programs," *Justice Quarterly* 14 (1997), pp. 145–66

42. T. David Evans and others, "Religion and Crime Reexamined: The Impact of Religion, Secular Controls, and Social Ecology on Adult Criminality," *Criminology* 33 (1995), pp. 211–12.

43. Patrick Fagan, "Why Religion Matters: The Impact of Religious Practice on Social Stability," *Backgrounder* 164 (Heritage Foundation, January 25, 1996).

44. Richard B. Freeman, "Who Escapes? The Relation of Church-Going and Other Background Factors to the Socio-Economic Performance of Black Male Youths From Inner-City Poverty Tracts," Working Paper 1656 (Cambridge: National Bureau of Economic Research, 1985).

45. David B. Larson and Byron Johnson, "Who Escapes? Revisited," final draft, 1998; Larson correspondence with author, September 1, 1998; Larson and Johnson, *Religion.*

46. Cynthia L. Sipe and Patricia Ma, *Support for Youth: A Profile of Three Communities* (Philadelphia: Public/Private Ventures, 1998), p. 31.

47. The one exception is the eighteen-to-twenty-year-olds of St. Petersburg, who spent only about a third of their after-school time in this way.

48. Ibid., p. ii.

49. Ibid., pp. 3, 81.

50. Michelle A. Gambone, *Launching a Resident-Driven Initiative: Community Change for Youth Development (CCYD) from Site Selection to Early Implementation* (Philadelphia: Public/Private Ventures, 1997).

51. Cynthia L. Sipe, *Mentoring: A Synthesis of P/PV's Research, 1988–1995* (Philadelphia: Public/Private Ventures, 1996).

52. Joseph P. Tierney and Jean Baldwin Grossman, *Making a Difference: An Impact Study of Big Brothers/Big Sisters* (Philadelphia: Public/Private Ventures, 1995).

53. Gary Walker, interview by author, June 1998.

54. Andrew Billingsley, "The Social Relevance of the Contemporary Black Church," *National Journal of Sociology* 8 (Summer-Winter, 1994), p. 3.

55. Harold Dean Trulear, interview by author, June 1998.

56. Glenn Loury and Linda Datcher Loury, "Not by Bread Alone," *Brookings Review* 15 (Winter 1997), pp. 13, 10–11.

57. Robert L. Woodson Sr., *The Triumphs of Joseph: How Today's Community Healers Are Reviving Our Streets and Neighborhoods* (Free Press, 1998).

58. See Jeremy White and Mary de Marcellus, *Faith-Based Outreach to At-Risk Youth in Washington, D.C.* (Center for Civic Innovation and Jeremiah Project, Manhattan Institute, 1998), pp. 1, 4, 6.

59. Tobi Jennifer Printz, *Faith-Based Service Providers in the Nation's Capital: Can They Do More?* (Washington, D.C.: Urban Institute, 1998).

60. Diane Cohen and A. Robert Jaeger, *Sacred Places at Risk* (Philadelphia: Partners for Sacred Places, 1998).

61. See Eric C. Lincoln and Lawrence H. Mamiya, *The Black Church in the African- American Experience* (Duke University Press, 1990), pp. 151, 15.

62. Naomi Ward and others, "Black Churches in Atlanta Reach out to the Community," *National Journal of Sociology* 8 (Summer-Winter, 1994), p. 59; Roger H. Rubin and others, "The Black Church and Adolescent Sexuality," *National Journal of Sociology* 8 (Summer-Winter 1994), pp. 131, 138.

63. See Harold Dean Trulear and Tony Carnes, "A Study of the Social Service Dimension of Theological Education Certificate Programs: The 1997 Theological Certificate Program Survey" (Ford Foundation, November 1, 1997), pp. 34, 40–41.

64. Greely, "The Other Civic America," p. 73.

65. Richard John Neuhaus, "The Public Square: A Continuing Survey of Religion and Public Life," *First Things* 81 (March 1998), pp. 63–65.

part five

Politics

eleven **American Racial and Ethnic Politics in the Twenty-First Century**

Jennifer L. Hochschild

The course of American racial and ethnic politics over the next few decades will depend not only on dynamics within the African American community but also on relations between African Americans and other racial or ethnic groups. Both are hard to predict. The key question within the black community involves the unfolding relationship between material success and attachment to the American polity. The imponderable in ethnic relations is how the increasing complexity of ethnic and racial coalitions and of ethnicity-related policy issues will affect African American political behavior. What makes prediction so difficult is not that there are no clear patterns in both areas. There are. But the current patterns are highly politically charged and therefore highly volatile and contingent on a lot of people's choices.

Material Success and Political Attachment

Today the United States has a thriving, if somewhat insecure, black middle class. By conventional measures of income, education, or occupation, at least a third of African Americans can be described as middle class, as compared with about half of whites. That is an astonishing—probably historically unprecedented—change from the early

1960s, when blacks enjoyed the "perverse equality" of almost uniform poverty, in which even the best-off blacks could seldom pass on their status to their children. Conversely, the depth of poverty among the poorest blacks is matched only by the length of its duration. Thus today there is greater disparity between the top fifth and the bottom fifth of African Americans, with regard to income, education, victimization by violence, occupational status, and participation in electoral politics, than between the top and bottom fifths of white Americans.

An observer from Mars might suppose that the black middle class would be highly gratified by its recent and dramatic rise in status and that persistently poor blacks would be frustrated and embittered by their unchanging or even worsening fate. Today's middle-class African Americans, however, express a "rage," to quote one popular writer, that has, paradoxically, grown along with their material holdings.[1] In the 1950s and 1960s, well-off African Americans frequently saw less racial discrimination, both generally and in their own lives, than did poor African Americans. Poor and poorly educated blacks were more likely than affluent or well-educated blacks to agree that "whites want to keep blacks down" rather than to help them or simply to leave them alone.[2] By the 1980s blacks with low status were perceiving *less* white hostility than were their higher-status counterparts.

More recent evidence confirms that affluent African Americans mistrust white society more than do poor African Americans. More college-educated blacks than black high school dropouts believe that it is true or might be true that "the government deliberately investigates black elected officials in order to discredit them," that "the government deliberately makes sure that drugs are easily available in poor black neighborhoods in order to harm black people," and that "the virus which causes AIDS was deliberately created in a laboratory in order to infect black people."[3] In a 1995 *Washington Post* survey, when asked whether "discrimination is the major reason for the economic and social ills blacks face," 84 percent of middle-class blacks, as against 66 percent of working-class and poor blacks, agreed.[4]

Ironically, most poor and working-class African Americans remain committed to what Gunnar Myrdal called "the great national suggestion" of the American creed.[5] That is a change; in the 1960s, fewer poor than well-off blacks agreed that "things are getting better . . . for Negroes in this country." In fact, defying logic and history, since the 1980s poor African Americans have been much more optimistic about the eventual success of the next generation of their race than have wealthy African Americans. They are more likely to agree that motivation and hard work produce success, and they are often touchingly gratified by their own or their children's progress.[6]

Assume for the moment that these two patterns, of "succeeding more and enjoying it less" for affluent African Americans, and "remaining under the spell of the great national suggestion" for poor African Americans, persist and grow even stronger. That suggests several questions for political actors.

It is virtually unprecedented for a newly successful group of Americans to grow more and more alienated from the mainstream polity as it attains more and more material success. One exception, a colleague notes, is South Carolina's plantation owners of the 1840s and 1850s. That frustrated group led a secessionist movement. What might embittered and resource-rich African Americans do? At this point the analogy breaks down: the secessionists' actions had no justification, whereas middle-class blacks have excellent reason to be intensely frustrated with the persistent, if subtle, racial barriers that they constantly meet. If more and more successful African Americans become more and more convinced of what Orlando Patterson calls "the homeostatic . . . principle of the . . . system of racial domination" (racism squelched in one place arises with renewed force in another), racial interactions in the political arena will be fraught with tension and antagonism over the next few decades.[7]

In that case, ironically, it may be working-class blacks' continued faith in the great national suggestion that lends stability to Americans' racial encounters. If most poor and working-class African Americans continue to care more about education, jobs, safe communities, and decent homes than about racial discrimination and antagonism per se, they may provide a counterbalance in the social arena to the political and cultural rage of the black middle class.

If these patterns should be reversed—thus returning us to the patterns of the 1960s—quite different political implications and questions would follow. For example, it is possible that the United States is approaching a benign tipping point, wherein enough blacks occupy prominent positions that whites no longer resist their success and blacks feel that American society sometimes accommodates them, instead of always the reverse. That point is closer than it ever has been in our history, simply because never before have there been enough successful blacks for whites to have to accommodate them. In that case, the wealth disparities between the races will decline as black executives accumulate capital. The need for affirmative action will decline as black students' SAT scores come to resemble those of whites with similar incomes. The need for majority-minority electoral districts will decline as whites discover that a black representative can represent them.

What of the other half of a reversion to the pattern of 1960s beliefs, when poor blacks mistrusted whites and well-off blacks, and saw little reason to believe that conventional political institutions were on their side? If that view were to return in full force among people now characterized by widespread ownership of firearms and isolation in communities with terrible schools and few job opportunities, there could indeed be a fire next time.

One can envision, of course, two other patterns: both wealthy and poor African Americans lose all faith; both wealthy and poor African Americans regain their faith that the American creed can be put into practice. The corresponding political implications are not hard to discern. The point is that the current pattern of political beliefs among African Americans is unusual and probably not stable. Political engagement and policy choices during the next few decades will determine whether affluent African Americans come to feel that their nation will allow them to enjoy the full social and psychological benefits of their material success and whether poor African Americans give up on a nation that has turned its back on them. Racial politics today are too complicated to predict if any trend, whether toward or away from equality and comity, will dominate. Political leaders' choices, and citizens' responses, are up for grabs.

Ethnic Coalitions and Antagonisms

America is once again a nation of immigrants, as a long series of news-paper stories and policy analyses remind us. Since 1990 the Los Ange-les metropolitan region has gained about a million residents, the New York region almost 400,000, and the Chicago region 360,000, almost all of them immigrants or births to immigrants. Most of the nation's fastest-growing cities are in the West and Southwest, and their growth is attributable to immigration. More than half of the residents of New York City are immigrants or children of immigrants. How will these demographic changes affect racial politics?

Projections show that the proportion of Americans who are neither white nor black will continue to increase, dramatically so in some regions. By 2030, whites (as currently understood) will become a smaller pro-portion of the total population of the nation as a whole, and their absolute numbers will begin to decrease. The black population, now just over 13 percent, will grow, but slowly. The number of Latinos, how-ever, will more than double, from 24 million in 1990 to almost 60 mil-lion in 2030 (absent a complete change in immigration laws). The proportion of Asian Americans will also double. (All of these projec-tions ignore intermarriage and changing definitions of races and ethnic groups.)

A few states will be especially transformed. By 2030 Florida's popu-lation is projected to double; by then its Anglo population, now about seven times as large as either the black or Hispanic population, will be only three or four times as large. Of 30 million Californians, 56 percent are Anglo, 26 percent Latino, 10 percent Asian, and 7 percent black. By 2020, when California's population could grow by as much as 20 mil-lion (10 million of them new immigrants), only 35 percent of its resi-dents are projected to be of European descent; 40 percent will be Hispanic, 17 percent Asian American, and 8 percent black.

These demographic changes may have less dramatic effects on U.S. racial politics than one might expect. First, the proportion of voters who are European is much higher than the proportion of the population that is European in states such as California and Florida, and that disproportion is likely to continue for some decades. Second, some cities, states, and even whole regions will remain largely unaffected by demographic change. Thus racial and ethnic politics below the national level will be quite variable, and even in the national government racial and ethnic politics will be diluted and constrained compared with the politics in states particularly affected by immigration. Third, most Latino and Asian immigrants are eager to learn English, to feel at home in the United States, and to be less insulated in ethnic communities, so their basic political framework may not differ much from that of native-born Americans.

Finally, there are no clear racial or ethnic differences on many political and policy issues; the fault lines lie elsewhere. For example, in the 1995 *Washington Post* survey mentioned earlier, whites, blacks, Latinos, and Asians showed similar levels of support for congressional action to limit tax breaks for business (under 40 percent), balance the budget (over 75 percent), reform medicare (about 55 percent), and cut personal income taxes (about 50 percent). Somewhat more variation existed in support for reforming the welfare system (around 75 percent support), and limiting affirmative action (around a third). The only issue that seriously divided survey participants was increased limits on abortion: 24 percent support among Asian Americans, 50 percent support among Hispanics, and 35 percent and 32 percent support among whites and blacks, respectively. Other surveys show similar levels of interethnic support for proposals to reduce crime, balance the federal budget, and improve public schooling.[8]

When political disputes and policy choices are posed, as they frequently are, along lines that allow for competition among racial or ethnic groups, the picture looks quite different, however. In the *Washington Post* survey, African Americans were overwhelmingly likely (82 percent) to describe their own group as the one that "faces the most discrimination in America today." Three in five Asian Americans agreed that blacks face the most discrimination, as did half of whites. But Latinos split evenly (42 percent to 40 percent) over whether to award African Americans or themselves this dubious honor. The same pattern appears in more specific questions about discrimination. Blacks were consistently more likely to see bias against their own race than against others in treatment by police, in media portrayals, in the criminal justice system, in promotion to management positions, and in the ability to get mortgages and credit loans. Latinos were split between blacks and their own group on all these questions. Whites saw roughly as much discrimination against all three of the nonwhite groups, and Asians varied across the issues.[9]

Perhaps the most telling indicator of the complexity in racial and ethnic politics is a 1994 National Conference survey asking respondents from the four major ethnic groups which other groups share the most and the least in common with their own group.[10] According to the survey, whites feel most in common with blacks, who feel little in common with whites. Blacks feel most in common with Latinos, who feel least in common with them. Latinos feel most in common with whites, who feel little in common with them. Asian Americans feel most in common with whites, who feel least in common with them. Each group is running after another, which is fleeing from it. If these results obtain in political activity, then American racial and ethnic politics in the twenty-first century are going to be interesting, to say the least.

Attitudes toward particular policy issues show even more clearly the instability of racial and ethnic coalitions. Hispanics support strong forms of affirmative action more than do Anglos and Asian Americans but sometimes less than do African Americans. In the 1995 *Washington Post* poll, whites were much more likely to agree strongly than were blacks, Asians, and Latinos that Congress should "limit affirmative action." But the converse belief—that Congress should not limit affirmative action— received considerable support only from African Americans. Across a variety of surveys, blacks were the most likely to support affirmative action for blacks; blacks and Latinos concurred frequently on weaker though still majority support for affirmative action for Latinos; and all groups concurred in lack of strong support for affirmative action for Asians.[11] Exit polls on California's Proposition 209 banning affirmative action found that 60 percent of white voters, 43 percent of Asian voters, and just over one-quarter of black and Latino voters supported the ban.[12]

What might seem a potential coalition between blacks and Latinos is likely to break down, however—as might the antagonism between blacks and whites—if the issue shifts from affirmative action to immigration policy. The data are too sparse to be certain of any conclusion, especially for Asian Americans, but Latinos and probably Asian Americans are more supportive of policies to encourage immigration and offer aid to immigrants than are African Americans and Anglos. A recent national poll by Princeton Survey Research Associates suggests why African Americans and whites resemble each other and differ from Latinos in their preferences for immigration policy: without exception they perceive the effects of immigration—on such things as crime, employment, culture, politics, and the quality of schools—to be less favorable than do Latinos.[13]

Taking Advantage of the Possibilities

We can only guess at this point about how the complicated politics of racial and ethnic competition and coalition building will connect with the equally complicated politics of middle-class black alienation and poor black marginality. These are quintessentially political questions; the economic and demographic trajectories merely set the conditions for an array of political possibilities, ranging from assimilation to a racial and ethnic cold war. I conclude only with the proposal that there is more room for racial and ethnic comity than we sometimes realize because most political issues cut across group lines; but achieving that comity will require the highly unlikely combination of strong leadership and sensitive negotiation.

Notes

1. Ellis Cose, *The Rage of a Privileged Class* (HarperCollins, 1993).

2. Jennifer L. Hochschild, *Facing Up to the American Dream: Race, Class, and the Soul of the Nation* (Princeton University Press, 1995), p. 74.

3. Ibid., p. 106; *New York Times*/CBS News poll, October 10–13, 1996, question 98.

4. *Washington Post*, Kaiser Foundation, and Harvard University, *The Four Americas: Government and Social Policy through the Eyes of America's Multi-racial and Multi-ethnic Society* (Washington, D.C.: 1995).

5. Gunnar Myrdal, *An American Dilemma: The Negro Problem and American Democracy* (Harper, 1944).

6. Hochschild, *Facing Up to the American Dream*, chap. 4

7. Orlando Patterson, "Toward a Study of Black America," *Dissent* (Fall 1989), pp. 476–86.

8. Jennifer L. Hochschild and Reuel Rogers, "Race Relations in a Diversifying Nation," in *New Directions: African Americans in a Diversifying Nation*, edited by James Jackson (Washington, D.C.: National Planning Association, 1999, forthcoming).

9. *Washington Post* and others, *The Four Americas*.

10. National Conference of Christians and Jews, *Taking America's Pulse: The Full Report of the National Conference Survey on Inter-Group Relations* (New York: 1994), pp. 3–75, 134, 136.

11. Charlotte Steeh and Maria Krysan, "The Polls—Trends: Affirmative Action and the Public, 1970–1995," *Public Opinion Quarterly* 60 (1996), pp. 128–58.

12. *Los Angeles Times*, "Elections '96 State Propositions: A Snapshot of Voters," November 7, 1998.

13. Princeton Survey Research Associates, "Immigration," *Polling Report*, August 11, 1997, p. 7.

twelve

The Unsteady March toward Racial Equality

Philip A. Klinkner
Rogers M. Smith

Under what circumstances does the United States make significant progress toward greater racial justice? We do not attempt here an elaborate empirical analysis of that question. Instead, we have combed through American history and arrived inductively at an answer that seems to us most likely. More rigorous testing by appropriate specialists should ensue, but we think it is also an answer worth describing before such investigations, as a possibility that all American citizens might usefully ponder. Though our case for our answer is only suggestive, it is disturbingly plausible. It is plausible because so much national history supports our argument. It is disturbing because if our answer is right, Americans must not only abandon the belief that there was anything inevitable about the overcoming of Jim Crow laws in the 1960s. They must also recognize that further progress toward overcoming racial divisions and inequalities is not likely in our time absent extraordinary efforts of a sort never undertaken before except under great duress.

This chapter is adapted from Philip A. Klinkner with Rogers M. Smith, *The Unsteady March: The Rise and Decline of America's Commitment to Racial Equality* (University of Chicago Press, 1999).

Our answer is that, at least so far in American history, substantial progress toward greater racial equality has come only

—in the wake of a large-scale war, requiring extensive mobilization of African Americans for success,

—when the nature of America's enemies has prompted American leaders to justify such wars and their attendant sacrifices by emphasizing the nation's inclusive, egalitarian, and democratic traditions,

—and when political protest movements prod national leaders to live up to that justificatory rhetoric by instituting domestic reforms.

We do not say that all these elements must always be present for progress to occur. We do say that, thus far, substantial progress has never occurred in their absence. All three elements have been at work in all three eras of significant progress toward greater racial equality in U.S. history.

The first reform era was the first Emancipation, following the Revolutionary War, when slavery was put on the path to extinction in the North and restrictions on free blacks and on manumissions lessened even in much of the South. The Revolution was fought in the name of republicanism and inalienable human rights against a monarchical foe, won with key contributions from American blacks, and accompanied by religious movements that highlighted the contradictions between the Declaration of Independence and the continuation of black slavery. The second era was during Reconstruction after a civil war that could not have been won without black soldiers. The resulting postwar constitutional amendments ended slavery and established formally equal black citizenship, in accordance with the strong demands of black and white abolitionists. The third period was the modern civil rights era, occurring in the wake of World War II and during the cold war and the Vietnam War, an extraordinarily prolonged period in which all three of the factors we stress were present. Throughout these years the United States mobilized huge numbers of black soldiers for actual or possible combat against Nazi and communist foes, against which American leaders stressed the nation's democratic ideals, while a broad array of civil rights protesters pushed them to make those ideals realities for all Americans.

After the first two reform eras, progress toward racial equality ceased in most, if not all, arenas of American life. Whites constructed new systems of racial hierarchy that significantly eroded previous advances. Today, after the fall of the Soviet Union and the end of the cold war, the forces that pressed for racial equality so powerfully for so long in modern American have receded, though not vanished. Whether the nation will continue to progress in that direction is, we think, the most important political question in America as the United States enters the twenty-first century. From our reading of the headlines of the present in light of the lessons of the past, we see abundant cause for concern.

The three pressures that produced the triumphs of the modern civil rights movement have now diminished. Though African Americans continue to serve disproportionately in the nation's military, the armed forces are now voluntary and reduced in numbers. The large-scale military mobilization of blacks during the cold war and Vietnam years is long past. Correspondingly, the United States does not have a clearly defined enemy against which it feels compelled to stress its comparatively democratic and inclusive traditions, even if it still does so in regard to some lesser rivals like Saddam Hussein and Slobodan Milosevic. There is also no large-scale civil rights movement pressuring the United States to live up to its more egalitarian ideals. Indeed, the largest mobilization of African Americans in the 1990s came with the Million Man March, organized by the separatist Nation of Islam leader Louis Farrakhan.

Though our argument will be uncongenial to many, no part of it is wholly original. Many black commentators, in particular, from the anti-slavery leader Frederick Douglass and the distinguished sociologist and historian W. E. B. Du Bois onward, have stressed the importance of war in motivating previous racial reforms. The historian John Higham has published a masterful brief analysis of the three reform eras just defined, which he calls "America's Three Reconstructions."[1] Higham similarly casts these major wars, and their accompanying defenses, in democratic, inclusive ideological terms, as vital catalysts to periods of racial progress, decisively reinforcing civil rights activism. He also worries, as we do, that the modern spirit of reform cannot be sustained without war's "moral equivalent." Higham is slightly more optimistic than we are about our current prospects, for he explains the sources of racial retrogression between these reconstructions somewhat differently.

Part of the explanation for the routine persistence of racial inequality interrupted by extraordinary periods of racial progress was offered by Du Bois.[2] Like him, we believe that the attachment of American whites to our country's long-standing racial ordering is not only, and perhaps even not chiefly, a matter of economic interests, though those interests are a major part of the story. Through most of our history, white Americans have also received a "psychological wage," to use Du Bois's term, from living in a society in which members of their racial group occupy the leading positions in most political, economic, cultural, and social institutions. That favored status has meant that whites are commonly accepted as the "normal" and norm-setting members of American society. People who have grown up within arrangements in which their group regularly receives special social esteem as well as more material benefits—arrangements that seem so familiar as to be virtually natural—are likely to find changes in those arrangements disquieting and to look for reasons to confine or condemn them.

Our fellow white Americans, we firmly believe, are not people inherently any more prone to racism, selfishness, or evil than any other group in this or any other society. Their attachments to familiar ways are perfectly normal and human, and in many regards such attachments can rightly be cherished. But in American society, whites have historically had the upper hand; thus many of their understandable attachments to the status quo have worked against overcoming real and severe injustices, despite genuine goodwill toward others. Even if there are economic benefits to be gained from egalitarian reforms, many whites consciously or unconsciously believe that any loss in the status they have long enjoyed is a cost too high to pay. Absent unusually strong imperatives to do so, most whites simply cannot be expected to pay that price. This privileged status of white people probably originated in the economic institution of chattel slavery, but it was embodied in virtually every institution of American life by the time of the Revolutionary War.

As political scientists we also insist that any analysis of prospects for reform in America ultimately has to come to grips with the incentives that shape the behavior of political parties, for little change can come without strong support from at least one major party. Even if powerful elements in American society support racial justice, no party is likely to push hard for it unless it can garner votes and dollars by doing so. Votes and dollars have always been predominantly in the hands of those who tend to resist change in arrangements that benefit them. For this reason, parties will normally have strong incentives to support racial justice symbolically, perhaps, but to eschew substantive change. Again, barring exceptional circumstances, we doubt that leaders of major political parties are likely today, any more than in the past, to champion policies that erode rather than reinforce the advantages of those groups that are most numerous, most affluent, and most politically powerful. The United States is a complex and diverse society, but middle-class and upper-class whites remain the best positioned. Indeed, the political advantages of whites have led political leaders past and present most often to uphold rather than condemn America's racial hierarchy.[3]

We must, of course, acknowledge that the American racial landscape stands vastly improved in many respects. The victories of the modern civil rights movement have transformed America. Most major institutions of American society—from military headquarters to legislative and judicial chambers to city halls to university classrooms to professional offices to corporate boardrooms—are more racially integrated than they have ever been. With those achievements the black middle class and, indeed, the black upper class have become far larger and more prosperous than in any previous era. Icons like Michael Jordan and Oprah Winfrey are hugely wealthy. And the civil rights movement's success in ending the national origins quota system in 1965 has meant that America has become more racially diverse than ever before, with fast-growing Latino and Asian populations transforming the traditional white-black, Euro-American–Afro-American structure of America's racial and ethnic composition.

Beyond these material changes, opinion polls suggest that whites have by and large abandoned their old beliefs in the legitimacy of racial hierarchies. Instead, the egalitarian ideals of the civil rights movement are celebrated in American discourse, institutions, and practices to a far greater degree than those of Reconstruction ever were. Martin Luther King Jr.'s birthday is a national holiday, and political leaders across the spectrum invoke his example in ways that were never true of Thaddeus Stevens or Frederick Douglass.

Blacks have indeed made great strides since the 1940s, and white attitudes have shifted in important ways. These changes, however, have resulted largely from pressures for racial progress that have now diminished. Although whenever these pressures have weakened, some important accomplishments have been sustained and analysts have proclaimed that racial problems are largely matters of the past, movement toward racial justice has then stalled and even receded.

Some argue, however, that the United States has reached a point at which Americans can expect continuing declines in racial animosities and the achievement of more equal opportunities for all, even in the absence of the factors that seem heretofore to have been necessary for real change to occur. Perhaps this is correct. On the other hand, we see abundant similarities between American political debates and developments in the late twentieth century and those of the late nineteenth century. Those similarities ought to restrain optimism that further racial progress will come automatically or easily. That the United States is not headed back to formal Jim Crow laws, much less slavery, is obvious. Beyond that, it is not so improbable that Americans of different races, and especially blacks and whites, will live in different regions, attend different schools, be concentrated in different occupations, and be governed by policies that reinforce these patterns, especially when they serve the interests and values of affluent whites and their closest allies. If so, the result is likely to be extensive de facto segregation accompanied by severe inequality in economic, educational, and political status and chronically fractious, sometimes explosive, racial and ethnic relations. This outcome is not improbable, because it is more or less where we are now and because the current policy discourse seems likely to move us further in that direction.

Racial Retrenchment: Historical Parallels

Though the number could reasonably be expanded or contracted in various ways, we identify here eleven significant similarities in the policy and political debates of the late nineteenth century and the current era. That seems to us too many to dismiss lightly.

The first parallel is the resurgence of arguments for state and local governance instead of national governance. The 1860s and the 1960s were both times of great expansion in the powers, size, and range of purposes of the U.S. government. During the Civil War and Reconstruction, the federal government undertook for the first time to promote racial legal equality and to punish racial discrimination and violence; to enfranchise African Americans, to make land and financial capital available to poorer Americans, white and black, on easy terms; to assist public education for all; and even to promote immigration and naturalization on a more racially inclusive basis. Similarly, in the 1960s, with the 1964 Civil Rights Act, the 1965 Voting Rights Act, the Elementary and Secondary Education Act, and the various elements of the War on Poverty program, the federal government acted on an even larger scale. Hence both eras saw dramatic shifts in power to the national level, shifts that could be objectionable even to those who did not oppose the purposes to which such power was being put—along with, of course, those who did.[4]

Each era then gave way to periods during which political leaders and the courts began declaring such expansive national governance to be inefficient and dangerous. Calls to recognize the democratic advantages of local government and for the sanctity of state's rights gained renewed currency, and many federal programs were limited or terminated. As support for radical Reconstruction waned, the Supreme Court began insisting, in the famous *Slaughter-House Cases* of 1873, that the postwar amendments must not be read as creating national powers so expansive as to "fetter and degrade the state governments" and make the Supreme Court a "perpetual censor" on state laws. Though this case did not involve any denials of black rights, later decisions such as the *Civil Rights Cases* of 1883 used such state's rights rhetoric, among other motifs, to achieve that end. Largely as a result of these cases, Congress based modern civil rights laws extensively on the commerce clause. In several dramatic recent cases, however, the Court has for the first time since the New Deal found limits on national commerce authority, invoking state prerogatives with a passion comparable to the majority in *Slaughter-House* and insisting with equal firmness that national civil rights guarantees are not thereby threatened. Chief Justice Rehnquist argued in *U.S.* v. *Lopez*, 1995, for example, that if the Court read federal power as expansively as the executive branch urged, "it is difficult to perceive any limitation on federal power, even in areas such as criminal law enforcement or education where States historically have been sovereign."[5]

Even more striking are the similar moves by policy advocates and political leaders in the reform parties of each era. Recall that Reconstruction crumbled after so-called liberal Republicans like Charles Francis Adams Sr. and Jr. abandoned the GOP rather than support continuing strong national measures. Today, many Democrats offer similar claims. Foremost among them is Bill Clinton. First as governor, and then as president, he has repeatedly endorsed claims that "centralized bureaucracies are no longer the best or most effective way to deliver services," that "the age of big government is over," and that we need a "new government" that is "smaller" and "does more with less." By the mid-1990s, voices urging more governmental activism had become, as in the late nineteenth century, virtually inaudible.[6] In fact, in 1996, Bill Clinton and a majority of congressional Democrats joined with the Republicans to end the federal government's sixty-year commitment to AFDC and to transfer it to the states.[7] This was the most significant devolution of federal power in memory, and it also ended one of the few national programs that had disproportionately aided racial and ethnic minorities.

The second similarity is the increased prominence of calls for governmental actions to be color-blind, resulting in the diminution of public measures consciously designed to assist racial minorities. Again the nineteenth-century Supreme Court provides a classic statement of this position: Justice Bradley's insistence in the 1883 *Civil Rights Cases* that, although African Americans had perhaps merited some assistance right after the end of slavery, "there must be some stage in the progress of his elevation when he takes the rank of mere citizen, and ceases to be the special favorite of the laws." Men like Charles Francis Adams Jr. also echoed that theme, contending that the "Afro-American" must accept "the common lot of mankind. He must not ask to be held up, or protected from outside."

Today, such calls are ubiquitous. A Supreme Court once receptive to affirmative action measures now says the Constitution demands "consistency of treatment regardless of the race of the burdened or benefited group." The former White House adviser and *American Prospect* editor Paul Starr has called for "race-neutral policies" on the ground, among others, that "affirmative action policies have helped to perpetuate racism." Similarly, the Democratic Leadership Council has repeatedly called for ending "quotas" and goals of "equal outcomes." It surely is possible that the late nineteenth-century calls to end special aid to blacks were premature, while the current ones are appropriate; yet there can be no denying that their content is remarkably similar.[8]

Supporters of color-blind and race-neutral policies point out that such efforts are consistent with the egalitarian demands of the civil rights movement, as represented by the Civil Rights Act of 1964. They fail, however, to acknowledge that some of the most racially discriminatory legislation meets their test of evenhandedness and racial neutrality. Poll taxes and literacy tests made no distinction according to race. Nonetheless, their clear purpose and result of such laws was to subjugate blacks to white rule. Furthermore, one can state that all efforts in American history to advance black equality—from state abolition laws to the Civil War constitutional amendments to the Civil and Voting Rights Acts of the 1960s—all violate some abstract notion of race neutrality since they afford blacks a degree of specific legal protection. Contemporary conservatives are increasingly making just that claim.

A third parallel, linked to both the antinational government and color-blind themes, is the resurgence of laissez-faire ideologies, which contend that private market forces will provide for more progress than public programs. The late nineteenth-century Gilded Age was notoriously the era of social Darwinism, intellectually led by men like Yale's first professor of sociology and political science, William Graham Sumner.

In the wake of the Reagan years, the similar resurgence of promarket ideologies among political leaders, policymakers, and academics requires no elaborate documentation here. It may suffice to note that conservatives like economist Thomas Sowell defend the claim that "market pressures are effective against discrimination," while government policies are not, by endorsing social Darwinian scholars like law professor Richard Epstein, who urges repeal of most economic regulatory legislation, including major portions of the 1964 Civil Rights Act. Epstein not only contends that governmental "protection against poverty increases the likelihood of its occurrence" but also grounds these claims in sociobiological evolutionary theories much like those Sumner invokes.[9]

Dinesh D'Souza takes these arguments a step further, calling for repeal of the Civil Rights Act's ban on private discrimination even though extensive racial discrimination could then prevail. He contends that it is after all "universal," "defensible and in some cases even admirable" to prefer "members of one's own group over strangers." Though at this writing support for the 1964 act nonetheless remains strong, in the wake of Epstein's urgings the Supreme Court has indeed heightened scrutiny of all government regulations in the name of protecting property rights against taking without just compensation. Epstein's positions still remain extreme, but again leading Democrats have shifted in the same direction. In 1991, candidate Bill Clinton urged that government be "reinvented" along the lines of "our greatest corporations," that government "monopoly decisions" be replaced by "more choice," and that we recognize that "work is the best social program this country has ever devised." Accordingly, as president he supported ending AFDC and called on the private sector to solve unemployment problems.[10]

Because people can and doubtless do oppose big government, affirmative action, government aid programs, and even federal antidiscrimination laws without harboring racism, the parallels so far may still seem undisturbing.

Consider then a fourth parallel: the resurgence of theories of nearly unalterable racial differences and inequalities, traced to both cultural and biological factors. The evolutionary theories of the late nineteenth century generally held that humanity had been socially and biologically formed into different races with sharply different capacities that could be altered, if at all, only over great stretches of time. For example, the anthropologist Daniel G. Brinton argued in his 1895 presidential address to the American Association for the Advancement of Science that the "black, the brown, and red races" had a "peculiar mental temperament which has become hereditary." Senator Henry Cabot Lodge argued similarly in urging immigration restrictions that year, contending that each race was defined "above all" by an "unconscious inheritance" of "moral characteristics" resulting from its distinctive history, upon which "argument has no effect." There was no alternative but to fence out any "lower race" that sought to come to America.[11]

Such views are not nearly so prevalent in the United States today, but since the end of the cold war they have become increasingly visible and respectable. Some modern accounts stress cultural differences in contrast to biological characteristics, whereas nineteenth-century writers tended to link the two closely; but cultural differences and inequalities often appear as ineradicable now as they did then and to have similar content. One important area where this pattern appears is in discussions of the so-called underclass, or ghetto ethno-underclass. Lawrence Fuchs argues that social analysts "commonly" use these terms to describe "a cluster of behaviors" that seem "almost foreign" to better-off Americans. These behaviors include unemployment among males, low labor force participation, drug abuse, criminality, welfare dependency, low-birth-weight babies; high rates of school dropout, teenage motherhood, single parenting, and female-headed households; and "distrust of mainstream institutions," including police, government officials, and employers.[12] These are, of course, the "behaviors" that so many stress in explaining black poverty today. Many analysts, moreover, dramatize the intractability of these traits in members of the underclass in ways that are disturbingly reminiscent of nineteenth-century arguments.

We should also mention the widely discussed book by Richard Herrnstein and Charles Murray, *The Bell Curve*, which argues that blacks are on average less intelligent than whites for partly genetic reasons. The *New York Times* science reporter Malcolm Browne claims that the *Bell Curve* makes a "strong case that America's population is becoming dangerously polarized between a smart, rich, educated elite and a population of unintelligent, poor and uneducated people." Such a possibility, Browne concludes, gives society the "right—perhaps even the duty—to strengthen our species' cognitive defenses against an increasingly dangerous global environment." *Newsweek* tells its readers that the book's research is "overwhelmingly mainstream" and that genetics accounts for up to 70 percent of the black-white IQ difference. The *National Review* recently featured a lengthy and flattering interview with Murray.[13]

Others echo these views. In a July 13, 1994, Senate hearing on welfare, New York Senator Daniel Patrick Moynihan said in regard to inner-city conditions, "I mean . . . if you were a biologist, you could find yourself talking about speciation here." Senator Jay Rockefeller of West Virginia replied, "when you were talking about a matter of potentially speciation, the creation of a new American person, so to speak, I think you're right about that." Senator Moynihan later apologized. A couple of weeks before that hearing, the nationally syndicated columnist and dean of the Washington press corps David Broder had approvingly quoted Moynihan's analysis of speciation, which Broder defines as "the impending creation of a different kind of human, one raised outside a father-mother setting."[14]

Most recently, Representative Bob Barr and Senate Majority Leader Trent Lott were linked to the Council of Conservative Citizens, a descendent of the white Citizens' Councils of the 1950s and 1960s and a group with decidedly racist views. According to one of the organization's leaders, "it is certainly true that in some important traits—intelligence, law-abidingness, sexual restraint, academic performance, resistance to disease—whites can be considered 'superior' to blacks." In 1991, Lott told a meeting of the council that it stood "for the right principles and the right philosophy."[15]

Claims that many blacks and Latinos are by culture or biology prone to lawlessness obviously reinforce *the fifth parallel: contentions that heightened governmental and community efforts to curb the "criminality" of racial and ethnic minorities are far more vital to progress than ending racial discrimination.* In 1905, Theodore Roosevelt was explicit on this point. "Laziness and shiftlessness," he wrote, "and above all, vice and criminality of every kind, are evils more potent for harm to the black race than all acts of oppression of white men put together. The colored man who fails to condemn crime in another colored man . . . is the worst enemy of his own people, as well as an enemy to all the people." Roosevelt called for "relentless and unceasing warfare against law-breaking black men."[16]

Contemporary policy analysts regularly strike a similar note, even though the United States now incarcerates a larger percentage of its population than any other nation except Russia, with black men disproportionately imprisoned; between one-fourth and one-third of all young black men are in some way under the control of the criminal justice system. The economist Glenn Loury believes that the incarceration rates of young black men, which might have been expected to fall during the 1980s as young men became a smaller percentage of both the black and white populations, were instead pushed even higher by the Reagan and Bush administrations' largely ineffective war on drugs.[17]

The sixth parallel has also already been suggested by the foregoing. As in the late nineteenth century, in the late twentieth century we hear increasing calls for immigration restriction. In both periods, much of the discussion centers on the economic consequences of immigration, with new immigrants viewed as too poor, uneducated, and unhealthy to be safely absorbed by the United States. These are legitimate worries, whatever the solutions. Further, in each period, concerns about the racial and ethnic character of the "new immigration" surfaced. It is true that such arguments were far more prominent at the turn of the century than they are currently; yet late nineteenth century advocates of race-based immigration restrictions did not fully prevail until well into the next century, with the 1924 National Origins Quota Act. Again, the visibility of such views is similarly rising today.[18]

It is thus striking that the 1924 act was immediately preceded by a prominent book that claimed to provide definitive scientific evidence for the turn-of-the-century racial theories like those of Henry Cabot Lodge and his fellow Yankee patrician, Madison Grant. The Princeton psychologist Carl Campbell Brigham observed in 1923 that

according to all evidence available . . . American intelligence is declining, and will proceed with an accelerating rate as the racial admixture becomes more and more extensive. The decline of American intelligence will be more rapid than the decline of the intelligence of European national groups, owing to the presence here of the Negro. These are the plain, if somewhat ugly, facts that our study shows. . . . The steps that should be taken to preserve or increase our present intellectual capacity must of course be dictated by science and not by political expediency. Immigration should not only be restrictive but highly selective.[19]

Those words smack of Peter Brimelow's views on the cultural imperatives justifying immigration restriction.[20] Near the end of their review of studies of American intelligence, *The Bell Curve*'s authors conclude that the "evidence that must also be acknowledged is that Latino and black immigrants are, at least in the short run, putting some downward pressure on the distribution of intelligence." As a result, they advise, America should "shift the flow of immigrants . . . toward those admitted under competency rules" because "present policy" cannot continue "without danger." No one has sounded this alarm louder than the Republican presidential candidate and national media commentator Patrick Buchanan, who once remarked: "I think God made all people good, but if we had to take a million immigrants in, say Zulus, next year, or Englishmen, and put them in Virginia, what group would be easier to assimilate and cause less problems?" In these comments the racial policy implications are perhaps not drawn quite so harshly (and again, many advocates of immigration restriction would not endorse these arguments). Once more, though, it is hard not to see similarities between past and present.[21]

The seventh parallel is an umbrella category that involves many developments, but in sum they amount to declining support and reduced federal efforts for effective civil rights enforcement. We have already noted that, in the late nineteenth century, Congress ended most of the Reconstruction programs aimed at securing greater racial equality, while the Supreme Court read the postwar amendments and civil rights statutes increasingly narrowly. From the second Grant administration on, moreover, even presidents of the party of Lincoln generally did not push for vigorous enforcement of those statutes and amendments. Eventually the federal government instead became actively supportive of state and local efforts to construct a Jim Crow system disfranchising and segregating black Americans in every state in which they formed a large percentage of the population.

Funding and staffing decisions by Congress and the president—as well as judicial rulings in areas such as the standing, removal, or appeal of cases from state to federal courts; standards of evidence in discrimination and desegregation cases; affirmative action; and other race-related matters—have meant that federal attempts to combat racial injustice have also diminished from end of the Carter years to the present. This decline has occurred despite studies showing continued high levels of discrimination in job and housing markets and despite residential and school segregation remaining high and, in some areas, increasing. Even so, as the Equal Employment Opportunity Commission (EEOC) has suffered funding and staff reductions, it has increasingly been unable to launch antidiscrimination class action suits, even when willing. The number of employment-related class action cases pursued by the commission fell from 1,174 in 1976 to a mere 68 in 1996. Although the 1991 Civil Rights Act did make employee discrimination cases easier to win, the reality remains that such activity is "one of the single most unsuccessful classes of litigation for plaintiffs," according to law professor Theodore Eisenberg.[22] Furthermore, since 1993, appointments to the nation's top civil rights post—assistant attorney general for civil rights—have been mired in controversy, forcing the position to remain empty for long periods of time.

Meanwhile, the Supreme Court has not just set the hurdles that must be met to justify affirmative action at unprecedentedly high levels, even for congressionally authorized affirmative action. It has also ruled that the burden of proof is now on those claiming existing school segregation is due to past de jure segregation, rather on those claiming that it is not, and it has indicated that it will not uphold even largely noncoercive judicial efforts to promote interdistrict desegregation in most instances. Yet as we have noted, influential conservative policy analysts are pushing to go even further, urging repeal of all or parts of the 1964 Civil Rights Act, the cornerstone of the second Reconstruction. Even if they do not ultimately succeed, such calls appear to be setting the tone of current policy debates far more than any advocacy of stronger civil rights enforcement. Moderate policy analysts such as the former White House deputy domestic policy director William Galston have endorsed the view that the "rights revolution" of the 1960s sparked changes that have "exacted a fearful toll," so that traditionalist calls "for a public change of course are not on their face implausible."[23] That very plausibility is, however, what makes it vital to attend closely to the racial consequences of enforcement cutbacks.

The eighth parallel is, fortunately, one of the less strong ones. It is the abandonment of electoral arrangements that have visibly empowered blacks. We often fail to recall sufficiently, however, that black disfranchisement came long after the demise of most Reconstruction programs. Because the Republican party remained preferable to the Democratic party in the minds of most African Americans, the GOP of the late nineteenth century had strong electoral incentives to continue to fight for black voting rights even after it had given up support for black interests in virtually all other regards. After a last-gasp Republican effort in 1890 to pass a National Elections bill not only failed but helped return democrat Grover Cleveland to the presidency, the GOP finally did surrender entirely on preserving black votes. Only then did disfranchising tactics proliferate. They were, moreover, indirect: literacy tests, Constitution tests, elaborate registration requirements, white primaries, the infamous grandfather clauses all allowed whites to limit the political power of blacks severely without openly denying blacks the vote on racial grounds.[24]

In contrast, the Voting Rights Act of 1965 has not only remained one of the most successful of the 1960s reform laws but has also been significantly strengthened, most importantly by 1992 amendments that overturned Supreme Court rulings and permitted litigation to focus on the racial consequences, rather than the intent, of electoral changes. That philosophy prompted the conscious creation of majority-minority districts after the 1990 census in areas where it appeared black voters rarely had meaningful opportunities to elect candidates of their choice. In states like North Carolina, Texas, and Georgia, new majority-minority districts were instrumental in electing minority candidates strongly favored by black and Latino voters. Indeed, such districts nearly doubled the number of black representatives and clearly helped create a Congress more integrated than any since the end of Reconstruction. The Supreme Court, departing from established precedents deferring to legislative districting even when done for openly partisan purposes, has firmly rejected the constitutionality of such districts in several major decisions, though. The black representatives elected in those districts have thus far still tended to be reelected, like most incumbents.

Many contend that black electoral influence will be greater with the end of deliberately crafted majority-minority districts. Abigail Thernstrom argues that those black interests may be better represented by (probably) white representatives in districts in which blacks are a significant minority than they would be by a black representative elected from a district in which they were predominant. In her view, representation by whites places blacks in a larger and presumably more effective coalition. The efficacy and desirability of majority-minority districts remains a genuinely difficult question on which unquestionably genuine champions of civil rights disagree. Still, the notion that we should prefer electoral arrangements in which whites are usually elected to represent blacks is not a new one in the United States, and its past record is not encouraging.[25]

The ninth parallel is the general abandonment of public efforts to achieve high-quality, integrated education for all residents. One of the most dramatic features of the first Reconstruction was the spread of schools in the South, both public and private, eagerly sought by an African American population starved for access to education. Many of those schools were integrated; indeed, even the University of South Carolina admitted both blacks and whites in the late 1860s. By the early 1870s, however, the waning of federal support for Reconstruction initiatives meant that not only did most public schools remain or become segregated but also some southern states began abandoning public schools altogether, with the result that in Louisiana, both black and white literacy declined during the 1880s.[26]

Today the Supreme Court has backed away from rigorous enforcement of school desegregation. Few white or black leaders champion school integration vigorously. Even the NAACP has recently debated whether to continue to uphold the cause of racially mixed schools or to accept the wisdom of striving for separate but equal institutions. The most discussed school reforms—such as voucher systems, or school choice, and reliance on private educational firms—are not aimed at providing integrated education for all and are more likely to carry de facto segregation even further. A Harvard study by Gary Orfield and others confirms that, abetted by the altered judicial rulings, school segregation has risen more rapidly during the the 1990s than at any time since *Brown v. Board of Education*. There is even growing support for de jure segregation in the form of calls by blacks as well as whites for separate schools to meet the "special needs" of young black males. It is unsurprising then that *Time* magazine in 1996 proclaimed the "end of integration," holding that a "four-decade effort is being abandoned." Though that assessment may be premature, there seems to be not a great deal more enthusiasm for integrated schools now than there was at the end of the first Reconstruction.[27]

The tenth parallel, closely linked to the turn away from the cause of integrated schools, is the heightened popularity of doctrines of black nationalism and separatism among African Americans. We have observed that the late nineteenth century was the heyday of Booker T. Washington, who publicly acquiesced in segregated schools and black disfranchisement when the Jim Crow system was being built. Blacks and whites could, he repeatedly assured all, be "separate as the fingers" in all their social and civil institutions while still working together harmoniously on matters of common interest. Marcus Garvey, inspired by Washington's example, came to the United States and built the largest mass organization of African Americans in history, the Universal Negro Improvement Association. The UNIA rejected integrationist goals and sought separate black economic, educational, and political institutions in the bitter belief that racial harmony was a pipedream, a belief most African Americans found all too plausible after World War I.[28]

In the wake of the Million Man March, one of the most visible African American leaders in the nation is Louis Farrakhan, head of the separatist Nation of Islam, an organization with roots in the Garvey movement. Farrakhan, to be sure, articulates a view not unlike W. E. B. Du Bois at certain times: eventually racial separatism will be overcome within a united humanity. For the foreseeable future, however, he insists that African Americans must be united with each other without any divisive outsider participating in their self-direction. The Nation accordingly supports separate black institutions in every sphere, much as the Garveyites did. The fact that many black Americans now seem to be drawn once again to a movement that regards integration as a damaging and quixotic goal suggests strongly that the politics of the current day display the loss of hope for a truly unified and egalitarian America that characterized the late nineteenth century.[29]

The eleventh similarity is that in both the late nineteenth and the late twentieth centuries, the political party that had led the reforms of the preceding era—the Republicans in the 1860s, the Democrats in the 1960s—did not explicitly abandon their professed commitment to their basic reform goals. They did, however, retreat to only passive support for those racially egalitarian goals, launching no further major initiatives to achieve them. Even after the infamous postelection bargaining with the South that allowed him to become president in 1877, Rutherford B. Hayes still went on to veto eight bills designed to weaken protection of blacks. His successors, James A. Garfield and Chester A. Arthur, each worked to enforce the Fifteenth Amendment guaranteeing black voting rights in certain strategic contexts, if rarely with any great vigor. It was not true even in a general political climate of retreat from Reconstruction that the Republicans did nothing to carry on its central cause.[30]

Similarly, modern Democrats can certainly claim to have resisted the most extreme efforts to undo the changes of the modern civil rights era. President Clinton has often spoken of his commitment to racial unity and healing, and he has sought to make a major initiative on race a central theme of his second term. Overall, however, the Democratic record on civil rights in the 1980s and 1990s, like that of the presidents Clinton admires in the late nineteenth century, has been one more of fairly passive resistance to conservative efforts rather than any strong positive program. When the Clinton administration has found itself linked with persons identified with strong civil rights activism, such as Lani Guinier, it has quickly severed those links. Its "mend it, don't end it" approach to affirmative action has not amounted to serious resistance to judicial and legislative efforts to do only the latter. Other examples could be adduced. Whether President Clinton's initiative on race will alter this pattern of resemblance to late nineteenth-century Republicans on race remains to be seen at this writing.

Policy Implications

Recognizing these similarities is, to be sure, only the beginning of adequate analysis of our current circumstances. The many differences between the circumstances at the beginning of the twentieth century and its end must equally be taken into account. A number of important conditions may well make continuing racial progress today easier to achieve than ever in our past. The most promising feature of the current context is America's continuing role as a world leader with the attendant necessity to appear fair in the eyes of nations of all racial and ethnic backgrounds. Even if racial and ethnic forms of nationalism continue to gain greater power and recognition in international politics, this leadership role will maintain pressure for the United States to treat all of its citizens justly. Additionally, the increasing interdependence of the United States and other economies and our reliance on favorable international trade agreements to promote economic growth, means that American policymakers will be reluctant to take actions that might alienate our commercial and treaty partners. Moreover, as long as economic arrangements permit the nation to achieve substantial overall economic growth, the disadvantaged are likely to gain some share of that enhanced prosperity, however unequal; and motives to scapegoat racial minorities will also be lessened. Finally, African Americans and other racial and ethnic minorities still have much more political and economic power relative to whites than they have ever had in our past, and despite the growing popularity of certain forms of separatism, they can be expected to use that power to combat truly invidious discriminatory policies forcefully. In light of these changes, it may not take a war to ensure continued progress.

It will, however, take far more than benign neglect. Recognizing that our current conditions have been massively shaped by a long history of political efforts to craft a hierarchical racial order and that there are impulses to do so again, we should ask ourselves how all proposed and current policies are likely to affect our inherited racial inequalities. If we think racial conflicts have been "America's constant curse," as President Clinton has argued, it is irresponsible and dangerous to fail to do so.[31]

To be sure, we would not require all governmental agencies to compile formal "racial impact statements" before promulgating regulations. We are not enthusiasts for bureaucracy or red tape any more than most Americans. However, we do think policymakers and analysts should mentally post on the walls facing their desks this question: If we go down this road, will we perpetuate or even intensify the racial inequalities that government has done so much to create in this country, or will we lessen them?

Notes

1. See John Higham, "America's Three Reconstructions," *New York Review of Books*, November 6, 1997, pp. 52-56. Higham believes that the American Revolution crystallized "a distinctive national ideology" of equal and inalienable individual rights and a dedication to the common good that has been the engine of the "enduring dynamics of racial reform" in America. Longtime organizing by reform groups, reinforced by the favorable milieu wrought by certain sorts of war, can sometimes drive the zeal of most Americans to realize these national ideals to heights that are expressed in substantial reforms. After their achievement, however, Higham sees moral fervor and national idealism fading and narrow economic self-interests coming to the fore, usually joined by racialist ideas justifying renewed inequalities. He believes, however, that if Americans can avoid undue cynicism about their failures and strengthen their faith in their original national ideals, the progress those principles have always supported can be continued.

2. W. E. B. Du Bois, *Black Resconstruction in America, 1860–1880* (Athaneum, 1992 [1935]), p. 700.

3. We are indebted here to Paul Frymer, *Uneasy Alliances: Race and Party Competition in America* (Princeton University Press, 1999). Also see Philip A. Klinkner, *The Losing Parties: Out-Party National Committees, 1956–1993* (Yale University Press, 1994).

4. Rogers M. Smith, *Civic Ideals: Conflicting Visions of Citizenship in U.S. History* (Yale University Press, 1997), pp. 277–83, 296–324.

5. Ibid., pp. 330–37, 375–76; *Slaughter-House Cases*, 83 U.S. 394 (1873); *Civil Rights Cases*, 109 U.S. 3 (1883).

6. Alice M. Rivlin, *Reviving the American Dream: The Economy, the States, and the Federal Government* (Brookings, 1992), pp. 9, 118, 126; Thomas Sowell, "The Right to Be Wrong," *Forbes*, June 17, 1996, p. 50; Democratic Leadership Council (Governor Bill Clinton, Chairman), *The New American Choice* (1991), p. 8; William J. Clinton, Second Inaugural Address, January 20, 1997.

7. In the final House vote on welfare reform, Democrats divided evenly, ninety-eight to ninety-eight. In the Senate, twenty-five Democrats voted in favor, with only twenty-one opposed to the bill.

8. Paul Starr, "Civil Reconstruction: What to Do without Affirmative Action," *American Prospect* (Winter 1992), pp. 9–10; Democratic Leadership Council, *The New American Choice*, p. 8.

9. Sowell, "Right to Be Wrong," p. 50; Richard A. Epstein, *Takings: Private Property and the Power of Eminent Domain* (Harvard University Press, 1985), pp. 320, 341; Epstein, "A Taste for Privacy? Evolution and the Emergence of a Naturalistic Ethic," *Journal of Legal Studies* 9 (1980), pp. 665–78.

10. Dinesh D'Souza, *The End of Racism: Principles for a Multiracial Society* (Free Press, 1995), pp. 544–45; *Dolan v. City of Tigard*, 114 S. Ct. 2309 (1994); Democratic Leadership Conference, *The New American Choice*, p. 5; Clinton, Second Inaugural.

11. Smith, *Civic Ideals*, pp. 355–56, 364–65, 410–19.

12. Lawrence H. Fuchs, *The American Kaleidoscope: Race, Ethnicity, and the Civic Culture* (University Press of New England, 1990), pp. 485–89.

13. Richard Herrnstein and Charles Murray, *The Bell Curve: Intelligence and Class Structure in American Life* (Free Press, 1994); Malcolm Browne, "What Is Intelligence and Who Has It?" *New York Times Book Review*, October 16, 1994, pp. 3, 41, 45; Geoffrey Cowley, "Testing the Science of Intelligence," *Newsweek*, October 24, 1994, pp. 55–60; Dan Seligman and Charles Murray, "As the Bell Curves," *National Review*, December 8, 1997.

14. Moynihan is quoted in *Newsday*, July 14, 1994; his apology is in a letter to the *Buffalo News*, August 2, 1994; David S. Broder, *Denver Post*, June 26, 1994.

15. Thomas B. Edsall, "Lott Renounces White 'Racialist' Group He Praised in 1992," *Washington Post*, December 16, 1998.

16. Theodore Roosevelt, "The Negro Problem," address to the Lincoln Dinner, Republican Club of New York City, February 13, 1905, in *The Works of Theodore Roosevelt*, Memorial Edition (Charles Scribner's, 1925), vol. 43, p. 445.

17. Glenn C. Loury, *One by One from the Inside Out: Essays and Reviews on Race and Responsibility in America* (Free Press, 1995), pp. 45, 72. Compare Loury, "The Conservative Line on Race," *Atlantic Monthly*, November 1997, pp. 148, 153; Loury, "An American Tragedy: The Legacy of Slavery Lingers in Our Cities' Ghettos," *Brookings Review* (Spring 1998), pp. 41–42.

18. Smith, *Civic Ideals*, pp. 357–69, 441–43.

19. Carl Campbell Brigham, *A Study of American Intelligence* (Princeton University Press, 1923), p. 210.

20. Peter Brimelow, *Alien Nation: Common Sense about America's Immigration Disaster* (Random House, 1995).

21. Herrnstein and Murray, *The Bell Curve*, pp. 360–61, 549.

22. Amy Saltzman, "Suppose They Sue? Why Companies Shouldn't Fret So Much about Bias Cases," *US News & World Report*, September 22, 1997, p. 69; see also Douglas S. Massey and Nancy A. Denton, *American Apartheid: Segregation and the Making of the Underclass* (Harvard University Press, 1993), pp. 4–16, 60–62, 96–109, 207–12; Ian Ayres, "Fair Driving: Gender and Race Discrimination in Retail Car Negotiations," *Harvard Law Review* 104 (1991), p. 817.

23. *Freeman v. Pitts*, 503 U.S. 467 (1992); *Missouri v. Jenkins*, 115 S. Ct. 2038 (1995); Richard Epstein, *Forbidden Grounds: The Case against Employment Discrimination Laws* (Harvard University Press, 1992); Sowell, "Right to Be Wrong," p. 50; Hernstein and Murray, *The Bell Curve*, pp. 447–508; William A. Galston, *Liberal Purposes: Goods, Virtues, and Diversity in the Liberal State* (Cambridge University Press, 1991), pp. 268–73, 287.

24. Smith, *Civic Ideals*, pp. 383–85, 451–53.

25. Abigail Thernstrom, *Whose Votes Count? Affirmative Action and Minority Voting Rights* (Harvard University Press, 1987), pp. 1–10, 208–15, 220–31.

26. Smith, *Civic Ideals*, pp. 320–24, 396–400, 464–68.

27. James S. Kunen, "The End of Integration: A Four-Decade Effort Is Being Abandoned as Exhausted Courts and Frustrated Blacks Dust off the Concept of 'Separate but Equal,'" *Time*, April 29, 1996, p. 38; Gary Orfield and others, "Deepening Segregation in American Public Schools" (Harvard Project on School Desegregation, April 5, 1997), p. 11; Peter Applebome, "Schools Experience Reemergence of 'Separate but Equal,'" *New York Times*, June 23, 1997.

28. Smith, *Civic Ideals*, pp. 417–18; Theodore G. Vincent, *Black Power and the Garvey Movement* (Berkeley: Ramparts, 1971).

29. For Farrakhan's views, see for example "Giving New Meaning to Race," from *The Final Call Online*, vol. 12, no. 24, 1996.

30. Rayford W. Logan, *The Betrayal of the Negro: From Rutherford B. Hayes to Woodrow Wilson* (Collier Books, 1965), pp. 43–45.

31. Clinton, Second Inaugural Address.

thirteen The Moral Basis of a Color-Blind Politics

Paul M. Sniderman
Edward G. Carmines

The civil rights movement targeted the legal apparatus enforcing the inferior status of black Americans. Fittingly, then the movement embraced the ideal of a truly color-blind society where, as Martin Luther King Jr. prophesied, our children would not be judged "by the color of their skin, but by the content of their character." The success of the civil rights movement, nearly everyone believed, marked the beginning of a historic journey to racial equality. Ironically, it marked the foundering of a historic public partnership between blacks and whites.

The partnership ran aground on several shoals, one of which was the call for black power and black separatism. Some civil rights organizations, once dedicated to whites and blacks working alongside one another in a common cause, expelled their white members as a matter of principle. Antiwhite rhetoric escalated, sometimes accompanied by calls for violence. As a form of symbolic politics, black separatism had a profound impact. Appeals to racial pride, nationalism, and solidarity took precedence. Integration as a moral idea was

This chapter is adapted from Paul M. Sniderman and Edward G. Carmines, *Reaching beyond Race* (Harvard University Press), by permission of the authors and reprinted by permission of the publisher, copyright © 1997 by the President and Fellows of Harvard College.

eclipsed, and the very idea of common ground between blacks and whites was widely rejected as an expression of white hegemony. Assertions of black autonomy, coupled with demands for white reparations, replaced arguments addressed to the conscience of white Americans. Stokely Carmichael's phrase, "Black Power," became a rallying cry.

Judged by the test of improving the objective conditions of life for blacks, black separatism made no difference. Judged by the standard of transforming the climate of opinion, however, it made a profound difference—unfortunately, for the worse. Failing to improve the lives of ordinary blacks, it succeeded in crippling the coalition most responsible for success in that very effort.

Black separatism is not the reason that America has a racial problem today. Its causes are a sticky compound of history and economics, made up of tenacious racial prejudice, the persistence of de facto racial segregation in housing and schooling, and the transformation of the American economy, including the withdrawal of semiskilled factory jobs from the inner cities. But although it is not the cause of America's racial problem, racial separatism has made it harder to solve.

Increasingly, whites who had played a central role in the civil rights struggle distanced themselves from the politics of race, not because they doubted the urgency of achieving black progress but because they were troubled, or angered, by the new spirit of separatism. Many of the most venomous battles over black power—for example, over community control of schools in New York's Ocean Hill–Brownsville—are now largely forgotten, but racial demagoguery continues.[1] The institutionalization of preferential treatment—on the back of civil rights laws passed on the strength of a pledge to treat everyone, white or black, alike—created a sense of betrayal and anger, as common on the left as on the right. Black and white Americans were driven even further apart. Political coalitions between blacks and whites shrunk. With civil rights laws on the books, a sympathetic Supreme Court to interpret them, and the Democratic party in control of Congress, it did not seem necessary to reach out to reconstruct an inclusive coalition for civil rights. American politics favors the status quo, and for a generation black political elites have been part of the political status quo.

Yet the objective conditions of life for many blacks have been getting steadily worse. The warning cry went out very nearly at the pinnacle of legislative success in the 1960s. America, the Kerner Commission declared, was threatening to split into two nations. One was white: educated, skilled, increasingly affluent, living under fair laws fairly administered. The other was black: embittered and alienated, victimized by poverty, crime, and social chaos, still caught in the coils of discrimination at the very moment they are proclaimed equal under the law. It was a nightmare vision. Preventing it from coming to pass has been the understood premise of informed American thought about race and public policy for a generation. The responsibility of those heading American political, educational, and economic institutions was conceived as making sure that blacks had opportunities now, not a generation from now. It was the need to ensure opportunity, not a commitment to an abstract doctrine of equality, that led so much of the nation's political elite to back public policies to overcome the racial divide.

Whatever else affirmative action policies have accomplished over the last quarter of a century, they have not brought black and white Americans together. Ironically, the urgent desire to reject the idea of two separate nations, black versus white, has persuaded many of the most thoughtful Americans of the necessity of racial separatism, at least temporarily. As Justice Harry Blackmun remarked in a now-famous formulation, "In order to get beyond racism, we must first take account of race."[2]

This premise of liberal thought on race has been motivated by a manifestly benign intent, a desire to see blacks better off. Yet, as the *Federalist Papers* argued long ago, democratic government can get into as much difficulty when it is in the hands of good men wishing to do good things as bad ones bent on harm. Convinced of the goodness of their objectives, advocates of race-conscious policies were inclined to view opposition as evidence of ill will. Far from being deterred by the inevitable clash of values—indeed, in part because they were aware that in any great enterprise a conflict of competing rights is unavoidable anyway—they swept forward.

In a society in which democratic citizenship matters, however, it is not enough for leaders to believe they are right nor enough even for them to be right. In the end, they must persuade the public that the goal they favor is worthy and that the means they make use of to accomplish it are fair. American political leadership has failed to persuade citizens that racial double standards are fair. It remains a conviction of the overwhelming majority of Americans that decisions about who should be hired, promoted, or admitted to college or professional school should be based on individual merit, not ethnicity. Hence, the largest part of their anger is aimed at racial double standards.

Advocates of a race-conscious politics dismiss the suggestion that America ought to pursue a color-blind politics. They charge that America is very far from color-blind and that turning a blind eye to the discrimination blacks still suffer and the disadvantages they still endure means turning the clock back. In their view, to proclaim that America must now be color-blind, with the job of ensuring equal opportunity no more than half done, will guarantee that America remains two nations, separate, hostile, and unequal.[3] Moreover, the argument runs, so far as differences in outlook and practices between blacks and whites are part of the constitutive diversity of American society itself, it is in everyone's interest, white and black, that race-conscious policies work. For example, we should ensure that no one getting a liberal arts education in the United States today can do so without seeing black faces or being exposed to black culture.

We are not unsympathetic to these concerns, but they must be judged by the evidence. Our research shows that race-conscious policies meet overwhelming opposition, with eight or more of every ten whites disagreeing with preferential treatment for blacks and at least one of every two angry or upset over it. Moreover the anger of white Americans over race preferences is not rooted in prejudice. On the contrary, it reflects in the main a conviction that effort and individual merit (as these have been and continue to be understood by the largest number of citizens, liberal or conservative) should decide who gets ahead. We have charted citizens' resentment and sense of betrayal. But even in the face of their anger over the turn taken by the politics of race and with all the opportunities that have been squandered, we argue that there is a still greater willingness to help those in need (including blacks) than has so far been acknowledged. More important, this support can be won for policies to help the worst off, very much including the worst-off blacks.

Much depends on the quality of the case made for policies to help the worst off. To win the most support requires the strongest arguments. Arguments that blacks deserve assistance because of the historic injustices done to them have a public constituency. Arguments that appeal to universal moral intuitions that go beyond race have more power, however—not because they ignore the moral aspects of race as an issue in American life but because they are the very foundation of Americans' moral understanding of race. For this reason, policies to help the worst off that now have the backing of only a minority can win the support of a majority, if we are willing to aim at a color-blind politics.

Is it true that the same policy framed in racially neutral terms gets markedly more public support than if it is formulated in racially specific ones? Suppose the answer is yes. Is the reason race prejudice? To get the most comprehensive view possible, we looked at public reactions to a number of different issues, among them enterprise zones, college scholarships, and school spending. To get the most reliable view possible, we made use of two independent surveys—the general social survey and the race and politics study. For each issue, a randomly selected half of the sample was asked whether they agreed or disagreed with a policy framed in racial terms; the other half was asked about the same policy framed in nonracial terms. For example, in the general social survey, half of the respondents were asked whether they supported or opposed giving business and industry special tax breaks "for locating in largely black areas"; the other half were asked whether they supported or opposed giving business and industry special tax breaks "for locating in poor and high unemployment areas."

Analogously, in the race and politics study, half of the respondents were asked if they would be willing to have their taxes raised a little "to improve educational opportunities for minorities"; the other half were asked if they would be willing to do so "to improve education in public schools." In all cases, then, we can assess the level of public support for government assistance specifically dedicated to blacks or on offer to anyone on the basis of need.

In these surveys, whites are markedly more likely to support a race-neutral policy than a race-specific one. Moreover, the difference for whites is significant, not just in narrowly statistical terms but also in politically practical ones. Take spending more money on schools. When help is restricted to minorities, only a minority of whites (46 percent) are willing to see their taxes raised a little; however, when the extra money is going to improve things for all public schoolchildren, then a clear majority (65 percent) are willing to do so.

Does this merely prove that a majority of whites favor a policy if they will benefit from it but oppose the same policy if only blacks will benefit from it? Our initial findings are certainly consistent with the possibility that race prejudice is at work; but they are also consistent with the possibility that policies advanced on universalistic grounds are more popular than those advanced on group-specific ones. What is needed is a direct test of both possibilities.

The School Tax Experiment

The school tax experiment starts with the premise that if prejudice really is the root factor undercutting support for strengthening educational opportunities for minorities (to take one example), then whites who dislike blacks should be more supportive of policies to help all schoolchildren than of those that concentrate on black schoolchildren; that is, the gap in levels of support among prejudiced whites should be large. Conversely, whites who like blacks should show less difference in their support of these two policies; their gap should be smaller.

In fact, the more positive that white attitudes are toward blacks, the bigger, not the smaller, is the gap between support for race-neutral and race-specific policies: 80 percent of whites who are least prejudiced support race-neutral policies, whereas only 50 percent of them support race-specific ones—a gap of thirty percentage points. Among the most prejudiced, on the other hand, the gap is much smaller. Quite simply, whites who dislike blacks are much less likely to support policies to help all schoolchildren than are whites who like blacks, a finding consistent with the consistent meanness of spirit characteristic of the prejudiced. Just because this meanness is general, not restricted to blacks, their racial prejudice cuts against supporting both versions of the policy, not just the race-centered one. Paradoxically, then, those who are racially tolerant, not those who are racially prejudiced, contribute disproportionately the winning advantage to policies formulated in racially neutral terms rather than in racially specific ones.

Perhaps, as William Julius Wilson suggests, whites are readier to support racially neutral policies rather than racially specific ones not because racially specific policies permit blacks to benefit but because they prohibit whites from doing the same.[4] According to this view, whites are reluctant to support race-centered policies because, though they too may need help from them, as whites they cannot get it. If whites object to government assistance policies targeted to blacks because they, as whites, cannot benefit, then whites who are most likely to benefit from such policies should be most likely to object. However we measure material interest, though—whether in terms of family income, self-assessment of financial condition, or security of employment status—it plays no consequential role in explaining why policies framed in racially inclusive terms are more popular than those framed in racially restrictive ones.

If it is not because of racism or self-interest, why are whites more likely to support a policy to help, for example, all schoolchildren (or all neighborhoods that are poor) than the same policy targeted at just black schoolchildren (or just black neighborhoods that are poor)?

A possible reason is this: aiming at all who have a legitimate claim to assistance has more appeal than singling out for special treatment only one specific and limited group among them. According to this view, what limits the appeal of racially targeted policies is not that they are targeted to benefiting blacks specifically but that they are restricted to benefiting a particular and limited group with a claim to assistance at the cost of neglecting others with the same claim. If this is right, then policies aimed at an equivalently particularistic group of whites should be similarly limited in their appeal.

The Helping Hand Experiment

To see if this is indeed so, we conducted the helping hand experiment. The key idea was to compare support for government assistance for blacks and for an equivalently particularized group of whites. As an example of a specific and limited group of whites, we chose "new immigrants from Europe." Designating them "from Europe" allowed us to identify them as white without using the potentially off-putting word "white." Describing them as "new immigrants" supplied a plausible basis for their needing government assistance. Whether referred to as blacks or new immigrants from Europe, they were described as "people having problems with poverty." If the skin color of the person getting the help is a crucial factor, whites should be more willing to help fellow whites. However, if the decisive consideration is that a specific and limited group is being singled out for help, there should be no difference in how white Americans react to appeals to help blacks and those to help a group of fellow whites.

To see which alternative is right, in the helping hand experiment a randomly selected half of the respondents were asked if they supported government assistance for blacks; the other half, if they supported government help for new immigrants from Europe. Strikingly, the race of the beneficiary does make a difference in whites' support for the policy but in exactly the opposite direction than the presumption of white racism would suggest. Whites are significantly *more*, not less, willing to give a helping hand to blacks than to fellow whites; specifically, 84 percent support help for blacks, 76 percent support help for whites. There is, in short, reason to believe that whites are less likely to support a policy restricted to blacks than one extended to both blacks and whites, because it is group exclusive rather than group inclusive.

Of course, in deciding whether to support or oppose a particular proposal for government assistance, who gets help is only one consideration that citizens may take into account. How they are to be helped also matters. Thus, whites are more likely to object if government assistance takes the form of welfare rather than, say, job training. Accordingly, the helping hand experiment was designed to take into account not only who is to be helped but also how they are to be helped. So in addition to, and independent of, experimentally varying whether whites or blacks were to be helped, half the time government assistance took the form of "welfare" and half the time "job training."

Arguments over government assistance are not just a matter of who is to be assisted or how they are to be assisted. They are also, we think fundamentally, arguments over why people should be helped. In the

American popular culture there is a belief that you ought to help people who have made an honest effort to help themselves but find themselves in need of help nonetheless. Accordingly, in a final complexity, half the time those who were to be helped were described as "people who show they want to work out their own problems" and half the time as "people who have trouble hanging on to jobs."

Both what kind of help was to be given and what people may have done to deserve it mattered. More whites favor government assistance if it takes the form of job training rather than welfare and if those who are to be helped tried to help themselves. Our real interest, however, was not in determining that either consideration mattered—we would have been astonished if they had not—but rather in establishing whether they counted the same for blacks as for whites. Specifically, are those who rely on government help more stigmatized in the eyes of whites when these recipients are black than when they are white?

Surely, common sense might lead us to suppose that stereotypes surrounding welfare have more onus attached to blacks than to whites, but this turns out to be one more case when common sense went awry. Judged in terms of support lost for government assistance, the charge that those who are getting help have not tried to help themselves cut just as deeply when applied to whites as when applied to blacks. Viewed the other way around, a reason to cheer is that blacks are given the same credit for individual effort and accomplishment as whites. Blacks get as much credit for trying to help themselves as whites, when all else is equal. The problem is that as a rule all else is not equal. When a group like blacks is perceived to benefit disproportionately from a program of government assistance *and* simultaneously is seen as not having tried to be self-reliant, there is a risk of being stigmatized. As a moment's reflection will make plain, the risk is not small but large.

Think of the "welfare mess." At its inception the centerpiece program, aid to families with dependent children (AFDC), aimed to assist women who, most often on account of the death of their husbands but in any event through no fault of their own, found themselves with the responsibility of raising small children alone but without enough money to do so. AFDC then had no racial character: it was about helping widows and small children, not blacks.

Much has changed since then. Seen through white eyes, welfare now has a black face. So, too, do crime and poverty. Blacks make up approximately 12 percent of the American population, or about one in every eight Americans. In our study, a majority of whites believe that an absolute majority of the poor are black, and an even larger majority of whites believe that an absolute majority of those arrested for violent crimes last year were black. Statistically, these estimates are wildly off, which demonstrates that ordinary Americans are not intuitive statisticians, not that they are unresponsive to reality. Race is a real problem in America partly because blacks are disproportionately likely to be poor, to be in need of AFDC, to be criminals, and to be victimized by criminals. It is this element of reality that drives the process of stigmatization.

Groups are at risk of being stigmatized if they come to be viewed as having been singled out, for a protracted period, for more than the ordinary measure of assistance. They are, moreover, at risk merely by virtue of being *perceived* to benefit disproportionately. The view of them as dependent on special assistance encourages a perception of them as undependable and lacking in initiative and self-reliance. Hence the danger of group stereotyping.

Just this danger is raised by the intersection of race and welfare in the minds of whites. Taking for granted that welfare is less popular than, say, job training, is it likely to be still less popular if its aim is to help blacks rather than whites? Translated into statistical terms, the question is whether the impact of describing government assistance as welfare is significantly larger when blacks are to benefit rather than whites. Our results are ambiguous. We can detect a tendency for welfare to be more unpopular when blacks rather than whites benefit, but strictly it is not statistically significant, hovering just above the conventional threshold.

Given this suggestion that something is happening, if not quite what we thought was happening, it is worth exploring the issue of stigmatization further. The race of the beneficiary of government assistance, taken in isolation from all other circumstances, may make no difference to whites, including those on the ideological right. When all the elements of the welfare mess—help in the form of welfare, which rebounds to the benefit of those who have not tried to help themselves and who are black besides—come together, however, things may change. Then race may become highly charged, especially for ideological conservatives—and this is just what happens. Even though conservatives respond quite negatively to the idea of welfare assistance for people who have proven themselves irresponsible, whether black or white, they respond still more negatively to blacks. By contrast, in the same circumstances, liberals are more likely to favor government help for blacks than for white immigrants, so far as they respond differently to the two. In short, the risk of racial stigmatization is real, not necessarily by the public as a whole but by the sizable portion of it on the political right.

White objections to policies restricted to blacks, it is now commonly argued, are rooted not just in prejudice and self-interest but often in group interest.[5] According to this view, whites oppose race-targeted policies not for the moral reasons they cite—for example, in the name of a color-blind society—but because whites cannot benefit from them.

An idea may be right even if its political consequences are wrong. The idea that the politics of race is fundamentally a matter of group interests, however, is both wrong and wrongheaded. Wrongheaded because, if the issue of race really were to reduce to group interests, given that blacks constitute only a small fraction of the citizenry, there never would have been a successful biracial effort in behalf of racial justice. Wrong because the coalition in pursuit of racial progress is potentially a political winner precisely because it is made up of both blacks and whites; indeed, in strictly numerical terms, made up principally of whites.

To be honest, we too fell into the trap we are now criticizing, underestimating the importance of moral arguments. What we realized, when we looked at the helping hand experiment in retrospect, is the importance of whether the argument made in behalf of a policy designed to assist blacks itself goes beyond race, invoking morally universalistic principles that apply regardless of race. To characterize the beneficiaries of a government policy as people who are in need and who have made an honest effort to deal with their problems on their own is to make a universalistic argument that they are deserving of help from others. It is universalistic because it applies across the board rather than being specially invoked in behalf of one group at the expense of another. What the helping hand experiment suggests, then, is that whites may be more willing to support race-specific policies if they are justified on universalistic, moral grounds.

Requiring blacks to drink from a water fountain marked "Colored" was morally wrong. It would have been morally wrong whoever bore the brunt of it, whether black Americans or Irish Americans, or Native Americans, or anyone else. What gave the civil rights movement its force was its insistence that discrimination on the basis of ethnicity violates our common humanity. Since the peak of the civil rights movement, the range of moral arguments advanced in behalf of a more decent society has narrowed. The test of whether racial policies are good has increasingly come to center on whether blacks will be better off as a result of them. That is a very important consideration but not the only one. Whether the means by which policies are to make blacks better off are fair also matters.

Speaking abstractly, no one would deny this. Consider, though, the practice of artificially increasing the civil service test scores of blacks by an amount necessary to ensure that a satisfactory number of them are hired or promoted. This practice of race norming, as it is called, turns the relation between ends and means on its head: since the end is desirable, namely, seeing that things are better for blacks, a once unimaginable means proves acceptable. In a liberal democracy, so arbitrary a practice cannot retain its moral character, however desirable its moral objective.

It is not only the means that have come to be contested. Once the moral high ground of American public life, the politics of race has increasingly taken on the character of interest group politics, because the values it serves have become increasingly particularistic. For example, much is made now of the value of ethnic diversity, with universities urged to select students and faculty and with businesses urged to hire and promote employees on the basis of their ethnicities. From the point of view of a politics that is both democratic and liberal, the issue is not whether diversity is a desirable state of affairs, worth making an effort to achieve, nor even that it is only one of many values. The problem is that it is a particular kind of value.

Diversity, when it means treating people who are similarly situated differently as opposed to valuing differences in people's experiences and outlooks, inevitably collides with the principle of equal treatment and the still deeper principle of equal worth. A claim to equal treatment and, still more fundamentally, to equal worth is preeminently a universalistic value; a claim to special treatment on the grounds of ethnicity is preeminently a particularistic value.

The problem is not that liberalism cannot offer good arguments in behalf of a particularistic value like ethnic diversity. The difficulty arises when diversity conflicts with a universalistic value like equal treatment under the law, as inevitably it does; then the arguments for particularistic benefits are not good enough. Hence the irony—and the accuracy— of liberalism's coming to be regarded as a philosophy of special interests. Liberalism's advocacy of ethnic diversity is rooted in principle, even in the face of its own political self-interest. Its very awareness that it is faithful to principle, sometimes to its own disadvantage, however, has blinded it to the fact that it has pledged itself to a principle that is—and in the end ought to be—subordinate to its own universalistic principles.

Although not all liberals reject an appeal for color-blind politics, nearly all who do reject it are liberals. In their judgment, to insist that our politics conform to a color-blind standard is to ensure that it will be color discriminatory. Some argue that race-conscious policies remain necessary on the grounds that race prejudice and discrimination remain a force. As Cornel West declares, "Given the history of this country, it is a virtual certainty that without affirmative action racial and sexual discrimination would return with a vengeance."[6]

Viewed objectively, to prophesy the return of racial and sexual discrimination "with a vengeance" is to take leave of the evidence, although it is important not to be distracted by polemical arguments and wind up neglecting better ones on which a critique of a color-blind politics can be grounded. The issue is not whether, if American policies were to aim at being color-blind, blacks will be treated worse than whites. It may be enough that they will then fare less well than now. After all, details of specific admission, hiring, and promotion schemes aside, the point of the structure of administrative regulations and judicial rulings now in place is to increase the probability that explicit and ample consideration be given to the needs and circumstances of blacks. If blacks lose their special status, if they become just one group among many in the kalei-doscope of American pluralism, is it unreasonable to fear that they will be lost in the shuffle? We respect the reasons for this concern, but we want nevertheless to suggest that if our politics committed itself to being color-blind, it would be to the advantage, not the disadvantage, of those blacks most in need of assistance.

Politics, from the perspective of citizens, is not so much about who gets what as it is about, more fundamentally, who *should* get what. The argument over race in public policy cannot be understood without real-izing that, in the eyes of citizens, it is a moral argument. What counts, for them, is not simply who is to benefit from government assistance; as important is why they should benefit.[7] The two are not the same, and if we are to see how possibly to move forward in the politics of race, they need to be kept straight.

Consider government assistance, say, in the form of job training. For argument's sake, suppose we are specifically interested in a policy to serve blacks and other minorities. Obviously, it is possible to urge its adop-tion on the grounds that blacks have historically been ill treated; and given the continuing legacy of prejudice and discrimination they suffer, it is appropriate that those among them who are out of work and who lack the skills to get a job receive some help in preparing themselves for employment. Indeed, this has become, for a generation now, the princi-pal line of argument in behalf of social welfare policies to assist blacks.

Yet exactly the same objective (to help blacks) through exactly the same means (by job training) can be advanced on grounds that are not restricted to or even centered on considerations of race. It is perfectly possible to argue that such programs of assistance merit support because those who are out of work and need to learn new skills to get a job and stand on their own feet deserve a helping hand, regardless of race. The same program can thus be argued for on two different grounds: that blacks ought to receive assistance given the price they have uniquely paid for being black; and more universalistically, that people who are in need of this kind of assistance should have a chance to benefit from it, and they should be able to do so independently of whether they happen to be black.

The Regardless-of-Race Experiment

We believe the current impasse over race can be broken. To see how, it is crucial to compare and contrast the power of these two different lines of argument, one confined to considerations of race and one that reaches beyond it: hence the regardless-of-race experiment. The experiment examines public support for job training programs. There are various reasons that public willingness to support programs like this matters. Perhaps the most important reason is that job training programs are part of an effort to help those most in need of help. Affirmative action, on the other hand, has the glamor of controversy but does not touch the lives of those who are worst off.

In the regardless-of-race experiment, the justification for government assistance varied. Half the time it was justified on the grounds that blacks have historically been mistreated; the other half of the time it was justified on grounds regardless of race. Always, whether the argument was confined to race or reached beyond it, blacks were to benefit. The purpose of the experiment was to see if public support for job training programs can be increased if the argument for government assistance goes beyond race, even though the policy is nonetheless restricted to blacks. Accordingly, a randomly selected half of the sample was asked:

As you may know, unemployment among blacks is high. Some people believe that the government in Washington should be responsible for providing job training to them *because of the historic injustices blacks have suffered*. Other people believe that the government is basically doing as much as it can and that it is now up to blacks to take care of their own problems. If you had to choose, would you say it is mostly the responsibility of the government to provide job training for blacks? Or is it mostly up to blacks to take care of their own problems?

Arguments, it is clear, were being made both for and against the program, but the central element in both was race. The remaining half of the sample was asked:

As you may know, unemployment among blacks is high. Some people believe that the government in Washington should be responsible for providing job training to them, not because they are black but *because the government ought to help people who are out of work and want to find a job, whether they're white or black.* Other people believe that the government is basically doing as much as it can and that it is now up to people, white or black, to take care of their own problems. If you had to chose, would you say it is mostly the responsibility of the government to provide job training for blacks? Or is it mostly up to blacks to take care of their own problems?

The political terms of reference remained exactly the same—job training programs run by the government in Washington, and the recipients of the benefits were clearly identified as black—but in the second case the arguments both pro and con were explicitly made regardless of race.

What difference does it make whether arguments for a policy stick to race or reach beyond it? Whites are approximately half again as likely to support job training programs for blacks if the policy argument, rather than being confined to narrowly racial grounds, is made on grounds that are universal, applying equally to blacks and whites. Specifically, whereas 21 percent of whites support job training when the appeal is racial, 34 percent support it when the appeal is universal.

To observe that a policy to help blacks wins the support of more whites if it is advanced on color-blind principles is not to say that it is guaranteed to win the backing of a majority of them. Certainly, in this instance it does not. Nor should this be surprising. Programs that restrict government assistance to blacks handicap their appeal to the public as a whole—and not because of racism. Moreover, even though arguments that reach beyond race are more effective than those restricted to it, it does not follow that a majority can be conjured up for a race-targeted program at will. Social welfare policies, like job training, are part of the deep cleavage over the proper role of government in America. They were contested before the issue of race moved to the center of public attention and, to a moral certainty, will remain contested when it recedes from attention.

Whether or not a supportive majority is guaranteed, the clear lesson of the regardless-of-race experiment is that it is better to make use of arguments that reach beyond race—to contend that help should be given because people are in need of it and can benefit from it, regardless of their race. For whom is it better? We think it is better for blacks. The cloud of cynicism blanketing the idea that our politics should be color-blind notwithstanding, precisely the point of the experiment is that even if policies target government assistance to blacks, it is still better to argue on grounds that reach beyond race.

There is another consideration at least as important as the level of support for programs argued on color-blind principles. What matters politically is not only how many voters can be won over by arguments that go beyond race but who they are. To begin with, support is boosted among liberals, the crucial core constituency for social welfare programs, by concentrating on color-blind principles. Only 40 percent of liberals support job training if the argument for the policy is restricted to considerations of race; but if it reaches beyond race, 55 percent support it. Conservatives, by contrast, cannot be rallied in support of programs like job training on whatever ground they are advocated, whether race specific or race neutral.

From a liberal perspective, the choice whether or not to support a job training program seems to reduce to whether or not one has the compassion and the willingness to sacrifice for others who are less fortunate. Just because the choice, so viewed, seems a matter of humanitarian values rather than political judgment, it is difficult for liberals to appreciate the sincerity of conservatives. So it regularly seems to the left that the resistance of the right must somehow be grounded in racial prejudice and that its objection to government assistance for blacks can be overcome, if indeed it can be overcome, only by shaming them into conceding that it is the right thing to do notwithstanding the fact that blacks are to benefit from it.

This misses entirely the merits viewed from the right and, by underestimating the sincerity of the conservative objection, underestimates its constancy. From a conservative perspective, Washington-run job training programs, however well intentioned, risk doing more harm than good, not only to the larger society but also to the very people they are ostensibly benefiting. Even though the objection from the right is political rather than racial, it cannot be blunted by reaching beyond race.

Ironically, then, the advantage of moving race politics onto a color-blind plane is not that it provides a way to escape politics, by shifting the argument over policies to a plane on which only moral considerations count, but rather that it provides a way to benefit from it. On the one side, if the argument for job training is made on the basis of values that are color-blind, support from the largest part of the public, which regards itself as free of ideological commitments, rises from 23 to 41 percent. On the other side, so too does support from that part of the public that regards itself as liberal. It thus pays twice over to argue on moral common ground.

These findings drive home the fact that the public's response to public policy can vary to a degree that matters politically, depending on the political argument itself. The strongest arguments in behalf of programs to deal with issues of race need not be confined to considerations of race. Indeed, the most effective way to increase the coalition in support of policies that directly improve the lives of the worst-off blacks is to reach beyond race itself, appealing to moral common ground and to principles that apply regardless of race.

An appeal to moral common ground would be less compelling if it were persuasive only among those most susceptible to influence—namely, the least well informed. In politics, persuasion of this form tends to be a Pyrrhic victory. If those most open to persuasion are the least well informed, the boost in support will be confined to persons least likely to act politically. However, the appeal of a universal argument is just as effective among those whose political understanding is high as it is among those whose grasp of politics is weak. For those concerned about the efficacy of a color-blind politics, this is a crucial finding. Since the most informed are as responsive as the least, there is reason to believe that *what* is being argued makes a difference.

The Color-Blind Experiment

The regardless-of-race experiment explored the politics of government assistance targeted by race but justified on grounds that reach beyond race.

What we examined here was the politics of policies that are color-blind with respect both to who is to be helped and why they should be helped.

In the last quarter of a century, both present circumstances and future prospects have dramatically improved for middle-class blacks; in contrast, the objective conditions of life for less-well-off blacks have deteriorated.[8] It is argued that the needs of better-off blacks should nonetheless remain at the center of public attention, since they are not yet as well off as well-off whites.[9] We proceed, however, on the assumption that, whether or not programs that primarily assist better-off blacks should be retained in place or not, primacy of attention now ought to go to those in need of assistance, including those who are both black and in need of assistance. Accordingly, we explore how much public support of social welfare policies can be boosted by making them color-blind through and through—that is, by ensuring that they aim at all in need, not just those who are black, *and* by making the case for assistance on the basis of a moral principle that goes beyond race, not just on the basis of appeals restricted to considerations of race.

The color-blind experiment was conducted to assess the calculus of public support for color-blind government assistance. The interviewer said to one of three people, randomly selected:

Some people believe that the government in Washington should be responsible for improving the social and economic conditions of blacks who are born into poverty. They say that because of the continuing legacy of slavery and discrimination we have a special obligation to help blacks to get ahead. Other people believe that the strength of the American way of life is that people should deal with their problems on their own. If you had to choose, would you say the government should take responsibility for improving the social and economic conditions of blacks who are born into poverty? Or should the government stay out of it?

In the first condition, then, the policy is targeted and justified on racial lines.

In the second condition, the argument remains the same in every respect but one. The interviewer said:

Some people believe that the government in Washington should be responsible for improving the social and economic condition of blacks who are born into poverty. They say that we ought to try to make sure that everyone has an equal opportunity to succeed. Other people believe that the strength of the American way of life is that people should deal with their problems on their own. If you had choose, would you say the government should take responsibility for improving the social and economic condition of blacks who are born into poverty? Or should the government stay out of it?

In the final condition, the beneficiaries of the program were broadened to include all people born into poverty, not just blacks specifically, *and* the justification for assistance was made on the universalistic grounds of equal opportunity, not one confined to issues of racial justice. Specifically, the issue was framed as follows:

Some people believe that the government in Washington should be responsible for improving the social and economic conditions of people who are born into poverty. They say that we ought to try to make sure that everyone has an equal opportunity to succeed. Other people believe that the strength of the American way of life is that people should deal with their problems on their own. If you had to choose, would you say the government should take responsibility for improving the social and economic conditions of people who are born into poverty? Or should the government stay out of it?

There is a politically significant gain in pursuing a color-blind politics. When the obligation to achieve equal opportunity is cast in narrowly racial terms (that is, when it is confined to assisting blacks and justified on the narrow ground of making up for the continuing legacy of slavery and discrimination), only 31 percent of whites agree that the government should take responsibility for improving the social and economic conditions of blacks. When the program is confined to helping blacks but justified not on racially specific but on morally universalistic grounds, then support for it goes up significantly, to 42 percent. But when assistance for those born into poverty is presented on genuinely color-blind terms, with neither its beneficiaries nor its justification restricted by race, one in every two whites back it. Of course, in gauging the strength of a political coalition, we need to take into account the public as a whole, minority as well as nonminority. Looking at citizens as a whole, when the issue of inequality is posed in universal terms and argued for on universal grounds, a decisive majority—57 percent— believes that government should take responsibility for improving the social and economic conditions of those born into poverty.

We are not suggesting that the politics of public policy is merely a matter of marketing. It is a matter of argument. The public's reaction to public policy hinges both on what is proposed by way of public action and on what arguments are made both for and against what is being proposed. Politics is very much a matter of argument and counterargument. What the experiment demonstrates is the strength of a color-blind appeal to the value of equal opportunity, not in isolation from other values but in head-to-head competition with the value of self-reliance. Our respondents had a real choice, with a potent value evoked on behalf of opposition to government assistance as well as in support of it. The fact that a majority could nonetheless be won for a truly color-blind politics thus offers a lesson most of us once knew but, perhaps because it was so simple, many of us have forgotten. An appeal to equality of opportunity gains strength if it is made on behalf of all equally, not on behalf of some selectively.

Why can whites more readily be persuaded to support policies that go beyond race? Surely, one possibility is that whites are willing to join and back a policy to help those born into poverty, on color-blind terms, precisely because it is *not* put in terms of helping blacks. On this view, color-blind politics are popular not because they appeal to a wider ideal but because they put out of sight the divisive ideal of racial justice.

To assess whether this view is correct or not, we attempted to gauge how committed whites are to the value of racial equality by taking account, simultaneously, of their views on a number of matters: the strength with which they reject a suggestion that we should give up the goal of racial equality "because blacks and whites are so very different"; whether they believe it is more important to promote traditional religious values in politics and society or racial harmony and equality between blacks and whites; and whether they think it is more important to maintain pride in and respect for our country or to promote racial harmony and equality between blacks and whites. If it is true that a color-blind politics owes its strength to its appeal to those unsympathetic to the value of racial equality, or even to those merely indifferent to it, then the impact of the variations in the color-blind experiment should be strongest for them; but we find that this is not true at all. Putting policy on a morally universalistic basis has as strong an appeal for those for whom the value of racial equality itself has the strongest appeal.

On the assumption that social welfare programs can effectively help those most in need of help, then a way forward is possible. Public support for these programs can be markedly boosted by making the argument for them on the basis of moral principles that cut across race; or by establishing that the objective of these programs is to help those in need of help, regardless of race; or both. Either approach gains adherents both among whites indifferent to the needs of blacks and among those genuinely concerned about them. If these policies are color-blind with respect to who should be helped and why, instead of enjoying the support of only a minority, they can win the backing of a majority.

Common Ground and the No-Special-Favors Experiment

One premise of a color-blind politics is that blacks and whites can join together in support of policies to assist those who are bad off, whether black or white, because they themselves share common ground not excluding issues of race. It is now more often presumed that when blacks and whites look at race they see two different realities, and in the light of the sensational stories that make headlines, this may seem self-evidently so. Although we are far from denying the genuine differences between black and white Americans, we believe it is worth the effort to see if there is also common ground.

We begin by underlining the differences between them, specifically with respect to the question of responsibility. As a first and very rough representation of the views of both blacks and whites as to why blacks remain worse off than whites, we asked both to assess blame: Are whites most to blame? Or are blacks? Or do both share the blame equally? Clearly, blacks and whites do not have the same view of the matter. Whites are twice as likely as blacks to believe that blacks are most to blame. To be sure, only a small fraction of either whites (20 percent) or blacks (9 percent) feel that blacks are most to blame; by contrast, far and away the largest number—two-thirds of whites and more than three-quarters of blacks—feel that blacks and whites are equally to blame.

Of course, a suggestion that both are to blame may have the superficial attraction of appearing evenhanded, and so, in an effort to understand more exactly what it might mean to say this, we investigated further the issue of blame and responsibility. Specifically, we asked those who think that whites are at least partly to blame if they think whites intentionally wish blacks to be worse off. That is, do whites try to keep blacks down? Or do they do it without meaning to? On this question, blacks and whites differ markedly. One of every two blacks (53 percent) say that whites try to keep blacks down on purpose, whereas only one of every four whites (28 percent) say that whites keep blacks down intentionally.

Having underlined that there are indeed differences, we believe that the best way to see if there is common ground is to allow blacks and whites the freedom to discuss the problem of race in their own words. Instead of requiring them to choose between alternatives that we define for them, we instead invited them to define the problem of racial inequality in terms they themselves chose, remarking to everyone that "statistics show that the average black person in America is worse off than the average white person" and then asking them, "What do you suppose caused this difference?"

In analyzing their answers, which were taken down as near to verbatim as possible, we categorized the reasons they gave for blacks being worse off than whites as finely as possible and then, so that the detail of their answers should not obscure their overall thrust, categorized their specific responses in larger, summary groupings. These summary groupings we organized under three headings: explanations that center on factors external to blacks, those that center on factors internal to them, and those that are tied to their immediate circumstances.

Our objective was to ensure that respondents were free to define the problem of racial inequality in their own terms instead of having to fit the round pegs of their ideas into the square holes of our point of view. All respondents were therefore free to mention as many different factors, of as many different kinds, as they wished.

Looking at the specific explanations that blacks and whites give when they are free to talk in their own words about why blacks are worse off than whites, we are struck by the similarity in their views. Blacks and whites are nearly equally likely to explain blacks being worse off than whites in terms of factors over which blacks have no control, among them inadequate schools and a lack of funding for education.

To say that their responses are similar is not to say that they are identical. For example, blacks are more likely than whites to point to a lack of economic—as distinct from educational—opportunity, while whites are more likely than blacks to attribute blacks being worse off to characteristics of blacks themselves, in particular to a lack of effort and motivation on the part of blacks. Whites are also more likely to point to the circumstances in which blacks find themselves, in particular, to problems within the black family. These differences, however, are a matter of degree. For example, just over one in five whites cite problems in the black family as part of the reason blacks remain worse off than whites; just over one in six blacks say the same thing. Moreover, both whites and blacks point to discrimination on the part of whites as part of the problem.

Recognizing the differences in emphasis, we are struck by the relative absence of racial polarization, the more so as our respondents were free to define the problem of racial inequality in their own terms, rather than having to confront it on ours. It is emphatically not the case that blacks see one reality of race and whites another, with blacks fixing the blame for blacks being worse off on whites and whites pointing the finger at blacks. On the contrary, most cite the same factors and to approximately the same degree. So far as they differ, the principal point of difference is the extent to which blacks, if they point to external factors, do so exclusively, while whites more often see a mix of factors, external and internal. What is striking is the amount of common ground between blacks and whites.

The impression of common ground is virtually absent from public discussion of race as an issue in American life. There is now a virtually unchallenged presumption that, looking at the issue of race, blacks and whites see altogether different realities. Certainly, this is what we expected to see—that is, after all, why we wanted them to be free to express their own point of view in their own words. But it is the similarity of blacks' and whites' views, not the dissimilarity, that stands out. We want, therefore, to take seriously the possibility that whites and blacks in America share more in common than is generally appreciated; and just because we ourselves wish to believe that they do, we have devised a specially demanding test to establish whether they do or not.

To say that a group of people—blacks, for example—should work their way up has become suspect. An insistence on self-reliance, it is now widely suspected, has become a symbolic cloak used by whites who dislike blacks to cover their prejudice politely. The underlying premise is that whites are applying to blacks a standard of conduct they would not apply to fellow whites. This premise is worth critical examination because the current overreadiness to make accusations of prejudice can distort values that whites and blacks hold in common.

In our no-special-favors experiment, half of all respondents (randomly selected) were asked if they agreed or disagreed (and whether they did so strongly or somewhat) with the following statement: "In the past, the Irish, the Italians, the Jews, and many other minorities overcame prejudice and worked their way up. Blacks should do the same without any special favors." The other half of the respondents were asked not about blacks but about "new immigrants from Europe," a designation deliberately chosen to make plain that the people being referred to are white, without explicitly saying so. In short, half of whites and half of blacks interviewed were asked whether blacks should work their way up, the other half of each group whether new immigrants from Europe should work their way up.

White respondents say overwhelmingly that blacks should work their way up, just as Italians and others have done, without any special favors. Whites are equally likely to believe that "new immigrants from Europe" should work their way up without any special favors. In short, to assert that whites expose themselves as racists when they declare that black Americans ought to work their way up without any special favors is false.

Now, consider the reactions of blacks. Cynicism about the commitment of Americans to a color-blind standard has increasingly itself become color-blind: if there is little faith that whites, free to choose between whites and blacks, will not favor whites, there is no stronger faith that blacks, free to choose between blacks and whites, will not favor blacks. Cynicism about blacks has been fueled not by systematic evidence on how ordinary blacks make up their minds—since the overriding fact is the dearth of information on what ordinary blacks think—but by highly publicized stories of individual black political figures who exhibit the failings characteristic of demagogues, whatever their color. Knowing little directly about ordinary blacks, even otherwise knowledgeable whites entertain the idea that when considerations of race are relevant, blacks will take a position primarily with an eye to whether it is advantageous to blacks.

Because of this cynicism, two aspects of the no-special-favors experiment are worth underlining. First, blacks, like whites, are overwhelmingly likely to believe that others—new immigrants from Europe, in this instance—ought to take responsibility for working their way up without any special favors. Second, and no less important, blacks are just as likely to believe that blacks should take responsibility for working their way up without any special favors as they are to believe that whites should do so. In short, black Americans also support the ethic of self-reliance and in a way that is altogether principled. Blacks are as willing to apply to themselves the requirements of independence and individual effort that they apply to others. For better and for worse, and to an extent that deserves appreciation, black Americans and white Americans share the same culture.

A Politics of Need, Not Race

A biracial coalition made progress possible in the past, and there will not be new policies put in place to help those who are in need, whether black or white, unless blacks and whites again make common cause. What our results demonstrate is that policies to assist those who are disadvantaged, even if they initially enjoy the support of only a minority, can attract the support of a majority, provided they aim to assist those who need assistance, whether black or white, and are advanced on grounds that apply regardless of race. It is by appealing to the values that black and white Americans hold in common that they will act in common.

To say that a commitment to a color-blind politics is worth undertaking is to call for a politics centered on the needs of those most in need. It is not to argue for a politics in which race is irrelevant but for one in which race is relevant so far as it is a gauge of need. Above all, it is to call for a politics that, because it is organized around moral principles that apply regardless of race, can be brought to bear with special force on the issue of race.

It will still be objected that a color-blind politics is possible only in a color-blind society. That gets the relationship between ideals and reality exactly the wrong way around. As Henry Bauer remarks, "Those who hold ideals, no matter that they are unattainable, are likely to behave more in accord with them than will people who do not hold those ideals."[10] We approach the reality of a color-blind society just so far as we commit ourselves to the ideal of one.

Notes

1. See for example Tamar Jacoby, *Someone Else's House: America's Unfinished Struggle for Integration* (Free Press, 1998), chapters 6, 7.

2. *Regents of the University of California v. Bakke*, 438 U.S. 265 (1978), p. 407.

3. See Andrew Hacker, *Two Nations: Black and White, Separate, Hostile and Unequal* (Scribners, 1992).

4. William Julius Wilson, *The Truly Disadvantaged: The Inner City, the Underclass, and Public Policy* (University of Chicago Press, 1997).

5. Lawrence Bobo and James R. Kluegel, "Opposition to Race Targeting: Self-Interest, Stratification Ideology, or Racial Attitudes?" *American Sociological Review* 58 (1993), pp. 443– 6.

6. Cornel West, *Race Matters* (Vintage, 1993), p. 64.

7. The distinction between who and why is analytical: the act of specifying a group to receive assistance—for example, disabled orphans (or less fancifully, blacks on welfare)—can implicitly present a reason for or against assistance.

8. See for example Gerald David Jaynes and Robin M. Williams Jr., eds., *A Common Destiny: Blacks and American Society* (National Academy Press, 1989).

9. See for example Ellis Cose, *The Rage of a Privileged Class* (HarperCollins, 1993).

10. Henry H. Bauer, *Scientific Literacy and the Myth of the Scientific Method* (University of Illinois Press, 1992), p. 39.

Contributors

Edward G. Carmines
Indiana University

Linda Darling-Hammond
Stanford University

John J. DiIulio Jr.
University of Pennsylvania

Christopher H. Foreman Jr.
Brookings Institution

Henry Louis Gates Jr.
Harvard University

Jay P. Greene
University of Texas, Austin

Nathan Glazer
Harvard University

Jennifer L. Hochschild
Princeton University

Christopher Jencks
Harvard University

Philip A. Klinkner
Hamilton College

Glenn C. Loury
Boston University

Orlando Patterson
Harvard University

Paul E. Peterson
Harvard University

Meredith Phillips
*University of California,
Los Angeles*

Rogers M. Smith
Yale University

Paul M. Sniderman
Stanford University

Abigail Thernstrom
Manhattan Institute

Stephan Thernstrom
Harvard University

Index